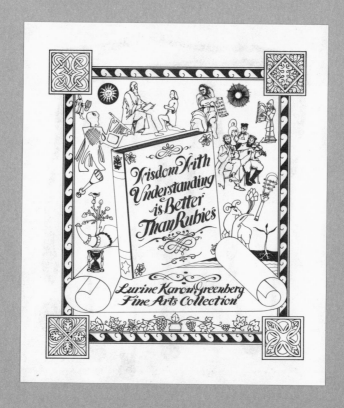

Aaron Copland's
America

Aaron Copland's
America

A Cultural Perspective

Gail Levin and Judith Tick

Watson-Guptill Publications

New York

Exhibition curated by

Gail Levin for

The Heckscher Museum of Art,

Huntington, New York

First published in New York in 2000 by Watson-Guptill
Publications, a division of BPI Communications, Inc.,
770 Broadway, New York, N.Y. 10003

Published in conjunction with the exhibition *Aaron
Copland's America: A Cultural Perspective* at
the Heckscher Museum of Art, Huntington, New York,
November 4, 2000—January 21, 2001, curated by Gail Levin.

Library of Congress Catalog Card Number: 00-107128

The text of this book is set in Electra, a serif typeface
designed in 1935 for the Mergenthaler Linotype Company
by the preeminent American typographer and book designer
William Addison Dwiggins (1880–1956).

Printed in Italy

1 2 3 4 5 / 04 03 02 01 00

Contents

FRONTISPIECE: *Gordon Parks (b. 1912)*, Aaron Copland. *Photograph, 1958. Copland Collection, Library of Congress, Washington, D.C.*

ACKNOWLEDGMENTS

A project as complex as this one succeeds only through the collaborative efforts of many people. The idea to commemorate Aaron Copland's centennial with an art exhibition came from Beth Levinthal, the curator of education at the Heckscher Museum of Art. At her invitation, I conceived the kind of show we might create. As I organized the actual exhibition, I have enjoyed working with her to develop the educational and audio-visual aspects of this project.

My interest in interdisciplinary scholarship prompted me to suggest the participation of musicologist Judith Tick, with whom I had previously collaborated. As a consultant, she has shared expertise and ideas, also contributing an essay on Copland's role in American and twentieth-century music.

I am especially grateful to the Heckscher Museum's director, John Coraor, for his enthusiastic support of my initial plan and generous response to all of the ensuing contingencies and needs. Conscientious work by Bill Titus, registrar, has been essential to the success of this endeavor. I have also received crucial aid and advice from Ann Cohen DePietro, the museum's chief curator. In addition I wish to thank Janie Welker, assistant curator, as well as Diedre Barrett, Nancy O'Brien, and others on the museum's staff who helped me in innumerable ways.

Baruch College of the City University of New York also facilitated these efforts. I am grateful to my colleagues in the Department of Fine and Performing Arts, especially Dennis Slavin and Virginia Smith. They encouraged my creation of a course that explored the relationship of art and music in twentieth-century New York, which benefited from my research for this project. Time off from teaching, including a fellowship leave, enabled me to complete this book. Leanne Zalewsky and Elizabeth Barry, two of my students at the Graduate Center of the City University of New York, assisted me with various aspects of this project.

I wish to thank James M. Kendrick of the Aaron Copland Fund for Music for permission to quote Copland's published and unpublished writing. The Heckscher Museum of Art is extremely grateful to the Copland Fund for a grant supporting its musical and educational programs. For help with the production of the audio guide, I wish to acknowledge the contribution of Stu Kuby of JSM Music. The Heckscher Museum of Art also thanks Boosey & Hawkes and ASCAP for their support of this project.

Michael Boriskin, artistic director of the Copland Heritage Association, has been important in many ways, including arranging for me to visit Copland's house in Cortlandt, New York, so that I could study what remains there of Copland's library and art collection.

I also appreciate the many others who have offered assistance and advice during the planning of this exhibition. Howard Pollack, whose authoritative biography of Copland was published after this project was well under way, generously offered valuable suggestions and read my essay in manuscript. The pioneering work of Vivian Perlis, who interviewed Copland extensively and collaborated with him on his autobiography, has also been essential. At the Library of Congress, which houses Copland's papers, Wilda Heiss was particularly helpful. I am grateful also to Vicky Risner and Raymond White at the Library.

The composer and conductor John Adams kindly allowed me to quote his penetrating observation on Aaron Copland and American culture. I am grateful, too, for the participation of several people who knew Copland, including Arthur

6

Berger, Rosamund Bernier, the late Rudy Burckhardt, Cornelia Foss, Lukas Foss, Richard Hennessy, Paul Jenkins, Buffie Johnson, Larry Rivers, Rhoda Sherbell, Erik Johns, and Edvard Lieber. The latter two have made available their drawings and photographs of Copland.

The generosity of many noted photographers and artists who captured Copland have helped to make this exhibition possible and reminded us of his memorable visage. We thank especially Arnold Newman, Gordon Parks, Irving Penn, and Naomi Savage, as well as the estates of George Platt Lynes, Hans Namuth, Ralph Steiner, and Carl Van Vechten.

Helpful advice from Larry Fleischer, Judith Guttman, Herb Liebowitz, Patrick Marnham, Cynthia Nadelman, Francis Naumann, Carol Oja, and Michael Rosenfeld (of Michael Rosenfeld Gallery) also benefited the project. We gratefully acknowledge all of the private and institutional lenders who have made this exhibition possible.

In addition I wish to thank Patricia Willis of the Beinecke Rare Book and Manuscript Library, Yale University; Linda Ferber and Barbara Dayer Gallati at the Brooklyn Museum of Art; Jennifer Vigil at the Cedar Rapids Art Museum; Dianne Nilsen at the Center for Creative Photography; Carter Foster at the Cleveland Museum of Art; Myron Kunin of Curtis Galleries; Ellen Sharp and MaryAnn Wilkinson at the Detroit Institute of Arts; Andrew Zeller of the AXA Gallery; Kathleen M. Ferres at the Grand Rapids Art Museum; Sharon Duane and Sally Morse-Majewski of Hancock Shaker Village; Amy Howe and Lynn Tondrick of the Isamu Noguchi Museum; Heather Lemonides of the Metropolitan Museum of Art; Darcie Alexander, Cathy Curry, Magdalena Dabrowski, John Harris, and Kirk Varnedoe at the Museum of Modern Art; Wendy Wick Reaves at the National Portrait Gallery; Kathy Goncharov of the New School University; at The New York Public Library: Julia Van Haaften of the Photography Division, Roberta Waddell of the Print Division, George Boziwick,

Phil Karg, and Grace Owen of the Performing Arts Division; Anthony Montoya of the Paul Strand Archive; Joseph Ketner of the Rose Art Museum, Brandeis University; Andrew Kelly and Leigh A. Morse at Salander O'Reilly Galleries; Laurette E. McCarthy of the Sheldon Swope Gallery; Lisa Dennison of the Solomon R. Guggenheim Museum; Dara Mitchell of Sotheby's; Andrew Lee of Tammiment Institute Library at New York University; Andrew H. Arnot of Tibor de Nagy Gallery; Betsy Kornhauser of the Wadsworth Atheneum; and Maxwell Anderson of the Whitney Museum of American Art. I also thank Charna and William Bloom, Alida Brill, Dr. and Mrs. Abraham Feingold, Suzanne Foley, Terry Geesken, Irwin Goldstein, M.D., Agnes Gund, Amy Hair, Joe LeSueur, Susan Lawrence, Mrs. Joseph Hirsch, Sarah Plimpton, Richard Rifkin, M.D., Alexander Rower, Bonnie Rychlak, Michael Scharf, Amy Schichtel, Bernarda Shahn, Edward Suckle, Jerry L. Thompson, and Judith K. Zilczer.

Judith Tick wishes to thank Northeastern University for its support of her work. In addition, she thanks Lawrence Buell, whose course "American Literature and the Environmental Imagination" suggested new ways to frame her ideas. Her essay also benefited from these readers: Jane Holtz Kay, Megan Marshall, Frances Malino, Lois Rudnick, Susan Quinn, and Larry Starr.

At Watson-Guptill Publications, it has been a privilege and a pleasure to have Marian Appellof as this book's editor; her carefulness and enthusiasm have greatly facilitated our work. Also appreciated are Harriet Pierce, Candace Raney, Bob Nirkind, Ellen Greene, and the book's designer, Derek Bacchus.

Finally, the project has enjoyed the enthusiastic support of Stephen Oleskey, Judith Tick's husband, and my husband, John Van Sickle, who as ever, has contributed invaluably and generously to my efforts from start to finish.

Gail Levin
New York City
July 17, 2000

7

Aaron Copland's America

Gail Levin

AARON COPLAND *reached his maturity at the same point that the country was seriously searching for its own cultural identity. Copland, like Robert Frost and Edward Hopper, found a way of expressing in the most simple and direct language deeply felt intuitions about the American experience.*

John Adams, Composer and Conductor, Aaron Copland Festival at Philharmonic Hall, New York City, December 4, 1999

A CENTURY FROM THE BIRTH of Aaron Copland, no one disputes that he helped create a distinctive American presence in classical music. Well known is the story of how a boy from Brooklyn, born of immigrant parents, discovered his musical calling early and launched himself into the ferment of his times. Yet his music and career have yet to be examined closely from a sufficiently broad cultural perspective. Through the lens of the visual arts, with a glance, too, at his interest in literature, this book and the exhibition it accompanies aim to reconstruct that broader context in which Copland thrived.

At every phase of his career, Copland enjoyed significant encounters with visual artists, critics, collectors, and dealers. Yet late in life, looking back to his time in Paris in the early 1920s, he would recall: "I knew the painters were very active, but I have never been as close to painting as to literature . . ."[1] He mentioned seeing "from afar" André Gide, Jean Cocteau, and James Joyce, "who made the biggest impression";[2] and he reflected, "If I had been more visual-minded I would have gone to many more exhibitions than I did."[3] Yet despite this comment, the important testimony here may be that he did indeed follow the visual arts.

LEFT: *George Platt Lynes (1907–1956), Aaron Copland. Photograph, gelatin silver print, 12 5/16 x 10 1/4" (31.3 x 26 cm), 1935. Copland Collection, Library of Congress, Washington, D.C.*

Copland's awareness of some of the major trends in painting is apparent from his use of visual metaphors. Discussing a piece by Charles Ives, *Central Park in the Dark*, Copland wrote, "The effect is almost that of musical cubism, since the music seems to exist independently on different planes. This so-called musical perspective makes use of musical realism in order to create an impressionistic effect."[4] On the other hand, cubist painters often made music their subject. For example, the American artist Max Weber, who picked up cubism from Picasso and Braque in Paris and showed briefly at Alfred Stieglitz's 291 gallery in New York, produced *The Cellist* (1917), a work that followed his publication, in 1914, of a book titled *Cubist Poems*.[5] When Copland described himself as using jazz "cubistically" to create greater intensity and excitement, he showed appreciation for the power achieved by painters in their experiments with multiple perspectives and simultaneity.[6]

A different sort of familiarity with the art world emerges when the name Pierre Matisse, a prominent New York art dealer and the son of the famed French artist, appears on Copland's guest list for a post-concert reception he was planning to hold at the home of a patron, Blanche Walton, in 1930.[7] This study will link Copland to many other figures in the visual and literary arts.

My inquiry has shown that there was much more exchange than has been realized heretofore between Copland and painters, sculptors, photographers, film-makers, critics, and an important architect. But beyond documenting little-known friendships and investigating the direct exchange of ideas among creative artists working concurrently in different fields, this book and exhibition also point to esthetic and intellectual parallels between Copland's music and the work of visual artists who were his contemporaries, independent of any personal acquaintance. It becomes ever clearer that Copland's remarkable talent developed in synergy with powerful concerns that shaped the times. He is most original, yet also most American, when he weaves into a distinctive modernist fabric the strains of folk and popular art, including jazz, amalgamated and transformed in a renewed classical matrix.

Max Weber (1881–1961), The Cellist. Oil on canvas, 20 1/8 x 16 1/8" (51.1 x 41 cm), 1917. Brooklyn Museum of Art, Gift of Mrs. Edward Rosenberg, 78.267.

Formative Years

AARON COPLAND WAS BORN IN BROOKLYN on November 14, 1900, the fifth and youngest child of Russian-Jewish immigrants.[8] His father, Harris, owned a successful Brooklyn department store and his mother, Sarah, assisted her husband with the business. As their youngest child, Aaron enjoyed the benefits of attention from his elder siblings, two of whom played musical instruments. It was his sister Laurine who first taught him how to play the piano, in the years before his parents consented to pay for lessons with a professional teacher.

The young Copland showed precocious interest in the cultural resources of Brooklyn and Manhattan. It is perhaps significant that the "first 'cultural' shock" he recalled experiencing was "the sight of a nude statue" at the Brooklyn Museum, a ten-minute walk from his home, when he was ten years old.[9] Just what he saw—a sculpture of a male or female figure—remains unknown, but installation photographs of the museum in that era reveal that casts of many sculptures from antiquity and the Renaissance were on view, including copies of Donatello's *David* and Giambologna's *Mercury*. He leaves unstated whether this early visual memory also reflected a growing awareness of his sexuality.

As a teenager Copland showed a natural attraction to new ideas. In the Brooklyn Public Library he read books by Sigmund Freud and Havelock Ellis. In music he discovered the French composers Ravel and Debussy and the Russian Scriabin. He vividly evoked his memory of attending, in 1919, what he described as "a recital by Leo Ornstein, considered *the* radical 'futurist' composer, whose *Danse Sauvage* was stirring up so much controversy."[10] (Although scholars have never specified, Copland appears to have heard the last of Ornstein's celebrated series of recitals, which took place on November 29, 1919, at the Aeolian Hall in New York.)[11] Besides *Danse Sauvage* (*Wild Men's Dance*) the program included works by Scriabin, Debussy, Ravel, Satie, and others.

Copland's recall of the controversial *Danse Sauvage* after so many years is especially revealing. That New York during the 1910s was home to many cultural and political radicals was not lost on Copland, who responded to challenges to the establishment. Ornstein, a Russian-Jewish émigré like Copland's parents, had been characterized as a "genuine Futurist," but also dubbed an "anarch" and denounced as an "agent for the spread of evil doctrines in musical art."[12] Anarchism in New York during the 1910s not only suggested Peter Kropotkin, Mikhail Bakunin, and other prominent political anarchists, but also became a metaphor to label philosophical anarchists who championed radical innovation in the arts. "Anarchistic" was used, for example, to describe the art of Vassily Kandinsky when his work was first shown in New York in 1912.[13] In the same vein, the photographer and art dealer Alfred Stieglitz was described in 1914 by the activist Hippolyte Havel as a "bombthrower" who "stands without doubt in the foremost rank. He is a most dangerous agitator . . . more than any other man he has helped to undermine old institutions . . . An iconoclast in the realm of art, he has succeeded in shocking cruelly the moral guardians of classicism."[14]

During this same period, the Ferrer School (or Center) in Manhattan, founded in 1911 by radical activists and named in memory of the executed Spanish anarchist Francisco Ferrer, coupled libertarian thinking with freedom in artistic expression. The center offered art classes led by such significant artists as Robert Henri and George Bellows. Among those who participated in the center's various activities were the modernists Man Ray and Max Weber, both of them, like Copland, the sons of Eastern European Jewish immigrants.[15]

Anarchy was a watchword and lightning rod, but Ornstein himself associated his work with yet another contemporary cultural agenda: the modernist search for what was then called "primitive." The primitivist used the idea of cultural difference in non-Western society as a means of subverting his own culture. Although this perspective presumes that the West is the dominant culture that will absorb the other, at the same time it suggests that non-Western culture offers some superior alternatives to the West.[16] Ornstein called the *Danse Sauvage* "a study in concrete rhythms," explaining, "What I tried to do was to write a dance so intense in expression that, though physically impossible of execution as a dance, it would call up to the listener on the wings of imagination the limitless strength and abandon of the nature dance in primal times!"[17] His music won praise from the critic Paul Rosenfeld in terms that make the cultural agenda clear; Rosenfeld describes Ornstein's work as evoking "the quality of the human experience there transmuted into sound" and remarks specifically on "its savage calls of the city to the one standing alone with the monument of a dead age."[18]

Ornstein's modernism intrigued visual artists. In 1917 his portrait was painted by Leon Kroll, who had earlier befriended the avant-garde artists Robert and Sonia Delaunay in Paris.

Leo Ornstein. Anonymous photograph, 1918. Private collection.

13

William Zorach (1887–1966), Leo Ornstein—Piano Concert. Oil on canvas,
30 x 24" (76.2 x 61 cm), 1918. Collection of Charna and William Bloom.

In 1918 William Zorach, a Jewish immigrant from Lithuania, painted *Leo Ornstein — Piano Concert*, seeking to express the excitement of avant-garde music on canvas. Zorach experimented with vivid color in ways that reflect his study in Paris from 1909 to 1911, during the midst of the fauvist period, when Matisse was the rage. At the same time, Zorach employed a compositional technique that repeats its motifs in the cubist fashion of Marcel Duchamp's *Nude Descending a Staircase* (1912), which had made such a splash at the New York Armory Show in 1913.

Ornstein's interest in African motifs, evidenced by his *Pygmy Suite op. 9* (1914), echoed Picasso and Matisse's earlier fascination with African sculpture.[19] And his search for a primal nature paralleled the fascination with African and Native American cultures felt by many artists and writers at the time who sought the directness and simplicity of what they saw as an earlier, less corrupt age. This was part of a larger struggle to counteract the growing sense of alienation and sterility in modern industrial society. Both American Indian and African art were mined for themes and motifs by such American artists as Zorach, Weber, and Man Ray, but also by Marsden Hartley, and writers such as Hart Crane, Vachel Lindsay, Langston Hughes, Jean Toomer, and Waldo Frank.[20]

Copland's attraction to modernist agendas would become for him in later years a point of pride: "I consciously hoped to forward the cause of contemporary American music by my activities and writings. If I was a leader in contemporary music, I was a follower of the modern movement in the other arts. As early as 1916, a group of writers began publishing *The Seven Arts*, a magazine conceived to promote their ideas."[21] Short-lived but influential, this modernist journal was founded as an American forum for radical ideas in the arts by the writer and poet James Oppenheim, who also published work by the novelist and critic Waldo Frank.[22] Copland's reference to it is especially significant, since its November 1916 issue featured a piece entitled "The American Composer," in which Paul Rosenfeld issued a ringing challenge to create "enthusiasm for American music,"

Alfred Stieglitz (1864–1946), Waldo Frank. Photograph, palladium print, 9 9/16 x 7 9/16" (24.3 x 19.2 cm), 1920. Metropolitan Museum of Art, New York, Alfred Stieglitz Collection, 28.128.2.

the dearth of which Rosenfeld attributed to "the American's lack of self-confidence that impels him to take his ideas and his art modestly and gratefully from Europe, and neglect his own."[23]

Copland credited both Frank and Rosenfeld for introducing him to the ideas and personalities of American modernism:

> Waldo Frank's book of 1919, *Our America*, challenged writers to
> bring America into the modern art movement. Alfred Stieglitz was
> the unofficial leader of this group. His gallery was the hang-out for
> younger artists such as photographer Paul Strand, painters John
> Marin and Georgia O'Keeffe (later Stieglitz's wife), Waldo Frank
> and other writers I met at Paul Rosenfeld's apartment.[24]

In *Our America*, Leo Ornstein merited Frank's attention: "Since there is no good American music save that of the Indians and Negroes, his music is as American as any. He calls it Hebrew. And he is right."[25] Claiming that "Walt Whitman would have loved the song of Leo Ornstein," Frank insisted on Ornstein's American quality.[26] Frank also celebrated the innovative role of Stieglitz's 291 gallery (which had closed in 1917). He called upon Americans to "prevail against the entrenchment of the Old" and lamented that in America, "The artist is still alone: his voice has not reverberated far. The call of the revolutionist is muffled."[27] In addition, *Our America* shows Frank to have been an early proponent of folk culture, a direction that Copland would explore.

Copland shared Frank's enthusiasm for Whitman, whose poetry he had discovered on his own at the Brooklyn Public Library, citing specifically "I Hear America Singing."[28]

> I hear America singing, the varied carols I hear,
> Those of mechanics, each one singing his as it should be blithe
> and strong,
> The carpenter singing his as he measures his plank or beam,
> The mason singing his as he makes ready for work, or leaves off work,
> The boatman singing what belongs to him in his boat, the deckhand
> singing on the steamboat deck,
> The shoemaker singing as he sits on his bench, the hatter singing as
> he stands,
> The wood-cutter's song, the ploughboy's on his way in the morning,
> or at noon intermission or at sundown,
> The delicious singing of the mother, or of the young wife at work, or
> of the girl sewing or washing,

15

Each singing what belongs to him or her and to none else,
The day what belongs to the day—at night the party of young fellows,
   robust, friendly,
Singing with open mouths their strong melodious songs.[29]

An analysis of Whitman's Americanism appeared in an article by James Oppenheim in the journal *The Dial* in January 1920; his commentary is notable for its insistence that a folk component would have made Whitman's achievement more substantial:

> Walt Whitman then gave us our first national art . . . he decided
> to take the only native expression we have, our conversation, and
> intensify it. The result is curious. Without the rootage of folk-song
> and folk-art there is a certain thinness, a loss of overtones. But
> there are real compensations—the work is, as I said, indubitably
> American, fresh, spacious, and free.[30]

Following the magazine's sale by the heirs of its founder, the January 1920 issue marked a new departure for *The Dial*, which had begun as a critical review in the Midwest, moving from Chicago to New York in 1918.[31] With a new editor, Scofield Thayer, and a new publisher, J. S. Watson Jr., the journal began to speak to a fresh generation of intellectuals.[32] It promised its readers "the best in all the arts" and "reproductions of the graphic and plastic arts . . . in every number." The visual arts selected included both American work and "the new and the old produced abroad."[33]

    The new *Dial* appealed to Copland's instinct for innovation and he added it to his preferred reading. He read its music critic, Paul Rosenfeld, on composers such as Arnold Schoenberg, Darius Milhaud, Igor Stravinsky, and Edgard Varèse. He read such modernist writers as Ezra Pound, E. E. Cummings, Hart Crane, and James Joyce. He saw reproductions of works by Pierre Bonnard, Marc Chagall, Henri Matisse, and Pablo Picasso, as well as those by artists working in America such as Stuart Davis, Elie Nadelman, and Gaston Lachaise. Copland's devotion to the magazine is evident in his letters home from France, where he went to study in 1921; he wrote repeatedly to his parents, imploring, "please don't forget to send me my magazine, 'The Dial'" and "keep on mailing the Dial once a month, please."[34] Popular with American artists, writers, and composers alike, the magazine was enshrined by Stuart Davis in his modernist canvas *Still Life with "Dial"* of 1922, where the beloved journal rests prominently on the tabletop of a cubist still life.

Stuart Davis (1894–1964), Still Life with "Dial." Oil on canvas,
49 ½ x 32" (125.7 x 81.3 cm), 1922. Private collection.

Study Abroad: The Parisian Avant-Garde

LIBERATION FROM THE OLD might be a cultural ideal, and America seemed to some the destined land of revolution, yet the way to excellence in music still lay in the Old World. Copland left for France in June 1921 to enroll in the American Conservatory of Music, a new summer school located at Fontainebleau. Aboard the *France*, the young American found himself seated next to a French painter, whom he described in a letter home as "a man of about 30" who "has been giving me the most valuable information about Paris."[35]

Copland later recalled that his new acquaintance conveyed a modernist point of view: "The painter was Marcel Duchamp. . . . Duchamp took a dim view of me trying to learn anything of importance about music, and especially the music of our time, at Fontainebleau. . . . I was terribly impressed by his independence of mind."[36] Copland, who probably did not know that, at the time, Duchamp supposedly had abandoned painting for chess, added that he had observed the artist on deck playing the game alone, as well as sitting "in a deck chair reading his book. He never looked out over the ocean."[37] Meeting Duchamp so thrilled Copland that he kept sending his parents bulletins. On his first day in Paris he reported, "I was quite alone as I had always been with the painter in the boat and not with the pupils of the school. The painter, by the way, is not coming to Paris until tomorrow and he has promised to call me up then. He has been very good to me and is exactly the sort of person I wanted to meet."[38] The letters to his parents give no sign that reading *The Dial* had prepared Copland to recognize his new acquaintance as a celebrated Dadaist well on his way to becoming one of the century's most influential artists.

The next day Copland reported, "Then my friend of the boat, the painter, came to Paris Monday and took me to a show. I expect to see him again before I leave Paris."[39] Years later in his autobiography, Copland recalled with obvious pleasure how Duchamp had gone out of his way for him, seeing him twice that first week, "treating" him to both a dinner and

Alfred Stieglitz, Marcel Duchamp. *Photograph, gelatin silver print, 7 7/8 x 7 1/2" (20 x 19 cm), 1923. Beinecke Rare Book and Manuscript Library, Yale University, New Haven.*

18

a show.[40] The unabashed enthusiasm of Copland's previous comments prompted his parents to inquire that fall what had become of the French painter. Their son answered, "Well, like all boat acquaintances I lost track of him. I think he intended to return to the U.S. by October anyway."[41] Copland's close friend and relative Harold Clurman (cofounder, with Lee Strasberg and Cheryl Crawford in 1931, of the influential Group Theatre) recounted in his own autobiography Copland's telling of how Duchamp had tried to discourage him, advising him to forget art and become a businessman like his father, exclaiming, "America is a place of business."[42] Clurman contended that Duchamp's words depressed Copland until he was able to convince his pal that although the French were "surfeited with culture . . . we Americans are *new*; we need art."[43]

What provoked Duchamp to take an interest in the young American composer may have been the important role that music played in his own family, who frequently staged musical performances like the one depicted in his painting *Sonata* of 1911. The composition shows his mother standing behind his three sisters—Suzanne in the foreground, Yvonne at the piano, and Magdeleine playing the violin. Musical imagery recurs in Duchamp's work, including his 1909–1910 *Musique de Chambre*, a cartoon of a man giving a young woman a piano lesson; a drawing, on lined paper intended for musical scores, of a bicyclist riding uphill on a tightrope entitled *avoir l'apprenti dans le soleil*, meaning "to have (which in French also sounds like the infinitive form of the verb 'to see') the apprentice in the sun"; and another piece, *Musical Erratum* (1913), that involved a randomly arranged sequence of twenty-five notes that he intended his sisters Yvonne and Magdeleine to perform.[44] Duchamp's interest in music is reflected as well in his notes; he wrote, for instance, "Construct one and several musical precision instruments which produce mechanically the *continuous* passage of one tone to another in order to be able to record without hearing them sculpted sound forms (against 'virtuosism,' and the physical division of sound which reminds one of the uselessness of the physical color theories.)"[45]

19

It was Copland's own antennae, however, not Duchamp, that immediately led the young composer to a center of modernist experiment in Paris, the Ballets Suédois. On his first night in Paris, he attended the company's premiere performance of *Les Mariés de la Tour Eiffel* (*The Wedding Party at the Eiffel Tower*), with a libretto by Jean Cocteau and music by Darius Milhaud, Georges Auric, Arthur Honegger, Francis Poulenc, and Germaine Tailleferre. Copland characteristically was struck by the modernity of the music and how it shocked the audience. He felt delighted "to get right into the action, where controversial music and dance were happening,"[46] just as he had witnessed the frisson of controversy over the music of Ornstein. Yet the budding modernist, despite Duchamp's scorn, kept to his plan of study at Fontainebleau.

Marcel Duchamp (1887–1968), Sonata. Oil on canvas, 57 x 44 ¹/₂" (144.8 x 113 cm), 1911. Philadelphia Museum of Art, Louise and Walter Arensberg Collection.

The summer course proved decisive for Copland's musical development, as it was there that he met and bonded with the renowned music teacher Nadia Boulanger, with whom he would study for the next three years in Paris. She would prove to be one of the major influences in his life, introducing him to outstanding musical figures of the time. By this stage of his education the young man had so thoroughly absorbed a modernist esthetic that sought to shock the public that after playing his own musical composition in the school concert, he wrote to his parents, "Sad to say, it made quite a hit; I say it is sad, because I can't get over the idea that if a thing is popular it can't be good."[47] Only the experience of the Great Depression of the 1930s would make him determined to compose more accessible music.

That autumn, after his stay at Fontainebleau, Copland settled in Paris, where modernism was in its glory. Many expatriate Americans were on the scene: the poet Ezra Pound; the painter Charles Demuth; the writer and art collector Gertrude Stein; the wealthy artists Gerald and Sara Murphy. Man Ray had just come from living in Greenwich Village, arriving in July 1921 and meeting up with his friend Duchamp, who had taken Copland under his wing just a month before.

Copland found quarters in Montparnasse with his fellow New Yorker Harold Clurman, who was studying drama and literature at the Sorbonne. "We were very serious about the arts," Clurman recalled, "but we had a lot of fun too, going around to places like Sylvia Beach's bookstore and catching glimpses of famous writers like Hemingway, Joyce, and Pound, and seeing the composers and poets in the cafés and restaurants."[48] He also wrote, "I learned a great deal about painting because we also knew painters," even boasting, "I made some discoveries before the regular art critics did, partly because of that early education in Paris."[49] Yet Clurman claimed that he went to the Louvre and most painting exhibitions alone, since "Aaron was admittedly insensible to graphic art."[50] Nonetheless, Copland could not have missed his roommate's constant talk about his new enthusiasms. Many of the new ideas in the air were shared by painters, writers, and composers. And Copland had his own treasured memories of the Parisian art world:

> Paris was filled with cosmopolitan artists from all over the world,
> many of whom had settled there as expatriates. It was the time of
> Tristan Tzara and Dada; the time of André Breton and surrealism . . .
> The painters were enormously active, with Picasso taking centerstage
> and interesting figures like Georges Braque and Max Ernst working
> in Paris at that time.[51]

21

In that environment, Copland conceived an interest in surrealism that would long persist. (Many years later Breton wrote an article for *Modern Music*, the quarterly review of the League of Composers, where Copland often published. This article may have inspired Copland to acquire one of Breton's books on surrealism, which he kept until his death.)[52]

The would-be American modernist found that his Parisian counterparts gave great importance to popular American culture, reinforcing voices Copland had heard already at home in Walt Whitman and from critics like Paul Rosenfeld and Waldo Frank. Paris's rage for things American moved Copland to remark to his parents that "in the Paris moving picture houses, I noticed that they advertised only American pictures, with Charles Ray and Norma Talmadge and Charlie Chaplin."[53] In November 1922, American expatriate Matthew Josephson, writing in the Dada magazine *Broom*, challenged Americans to create an indigenous art by drawing on their own popular culture; the artist needed to "plunge hardily into that effervescent revolving cacophonous milieu . . . where the Billposters enunciate their wisdom, the Cinemas transport us, the newspapers intone their gaudy jargon . . . and skyscrapers rise lyrically to the exotic rhythm of jazz bands."[54]

The Influence of Jazz

AMONG ALL THE STRAINS OF AMERICAN POPULAR CULTURE, it was jazz that most fascinated and transformed the imagination across the arts on both sides of the Atlantic. As early as the mid-1910s Charles Demuth, a fan of New York's African-American cabarets featuring ragtime and jazz, was painting scenes from this milieu. Among these are his watercolors called *At Marshall's* (named for a club he especially favored, a gathering place for black and white artists and intellectuals that was located in the basement of the Marshall Hotel on West Fifty-third Street, under the Sixth Avenue El), *Negro Jazz Band*, *The Jazz Singer*, and *Negro Girl Dancing*.[55] And Man Ray, in New York during that time, followed his canvas *Symphony Orchestra* of 1916 with *Jazz* (1919), an abstraction on paper done with an airbrush. In the earlier work he depicted the flattened forms of musical instruments seen from directly above; in *Jazz*, a keyboard is superimposed across more organic shapes, which now appear less recognizable as instruments and seem to give form to sounds.

22

The 1920s in New York brought the Harlem Renaissance, a flowering of African-American culture that reached well beyond African-American audiences to attract patrons like Copland's friend Carl Van Vechten, a music and dance critic, photographer, and novelist. Jazz, a big part of this cultural phenomenon, enchanted artists from abroad. Duchamp recalled Demuth's taking him to a club in Harlem for the first time.[56] The French artists Francis Picabia and Albert Gleizes, both of whom worked for a while in New York, also admired and made allusions to jazz in paintings they produced there during the 1910s. John Marin, who, like Demuth, showed with Stieglitz, felt the influence of jazz too, which is reflected in such works as his watercolor *Broadway Night* (1929) and his canvas

*Charles Demuth (1883–1935), The Jazz Singer.
Watercolor on paper, 12 ⅞ x 7 ⅞" (37.2. x 20 cm),
1916. Private collection.*

Charles Demuth, Negro Jazz Band. Watercolor on paper,
12 ⅞ x 7 ⅞" (37.2 x 20 cm), 1916. Collection of Dr. and Mrs. Irwin Goldstein.

Man Ray (1890–1976), Jazz. Aerograph, tempera and ink on paper, 27 x 21" (68.6 x 53.3 cm), 1919.
Columbus Museum of Art, Ohio, Gift of Ferdinand Howland.

25

John Marin (1870–1953), Mid-Manhattan No. 2.
Oil on canvas, 35 x 26" (88.9 x 66 cm), 1932. The Regis Collection, Minneapolis.

Mid-Manhattan No. 2 (1932). In the latter, Marin created the illusion of rhythmic jazz movement through the repetition of zigzag lines in the upper right and through the blurred crowd of pedestrians crossing the street in the foreground. In 1924, well in advance of producing this work, he wrote to Stieglitz about his view of "the land of jazz—lights and movies—the land of the moneyspenders,"[57] a notion that strongly recalls the themes of Gerald Murphy and Cole Porter's ballet *Within the Quota*, which had just traveled to New York from Paris.[58]

The African-American music of New York became so fashionable in Paris during the early 1920s that the American poet Alfred Kreymborg wrote, "Vaudeville, the latest Argentinean tango, American jazz, skyscrapers, machinery, advertising methods—these were the new gods here."[59] *Within the Quota*, the "American" ballet Gerald Murphy conceived for the Ballets Suédois in 1923, incorporated jazz-inspired music by Cole Porter. Murphy, who not only wrote the scenario but also designed the sets and costumes, created a character known as the "Jazzbaby," a sultry woman in a slinky gown.[60] Copland, we know, saw this ballet, since it was performed along with one that he described as "the most charming of the [Milhaud] ballets," *La Création du Monde*. Along with its music by Darius Milhaud, who had heard jazz in Harlem in 1922, the production featured a libretto by Blaise Cendrars and African-inspired sets and costumes designed by Fernand Léger.[61] Léger's sets transformed shapes of African sculpture as if seen through a cubist prism. Copland recalled *La Création du Monde* in terms that reveal his own deep interest in jazz:

Set and costumes by Fernand Léger (1881–1955) for La Création du Monde,
Ballets Suédois production, 1923. Anonymous photograph. Courtesy Dansmuseet, Stockholm.

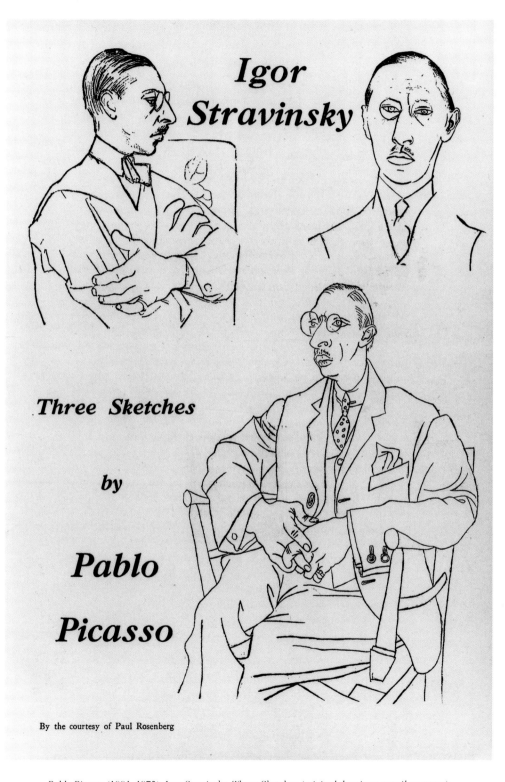

Igor Stravinsky

Three Sketches

by

Pablo Picasso

By the courtesy of Paul Rosenberg

Pablo Picasso (1881–1973), Igor Stravinsky, Three Sketches (original drawings: pencil on paper).
Published in The League of Composers Review, New York, February 1924. ©2000 Estate of Pablo
Picasso/Artists Rights Society (ARS), New York.

Much of the music is lifted from jazz—there are fugues on a jazz subject, a blues section, and a long melody over a "barbershop" accompaniment. Better than any other European, and before hearing Gershwin's famous Rhapsody (first performed in the following year), Milhaud understood how to assimilate jazz idiom.[62]

The ballet, Copland also remarked, treated "the creation of the world according to African legends." It recalled the Africanism of Ornstein that Copland had heard in New York and confirmed the imaginative link between jazz and the larger cultural search for what modernists viewed as primitive. More readily than many Americans, Milhaud and other European composers and critics admired the jazz music of black Americans as avant-garde and wonderfully exotic instead of threatening, just as vanguard artists such as Matisse, Picasso, and Léger had embraced African sculpture. Copland was familiar with ragtime and popular music from Brooklyn; he even recalled the piles of ragtime sheet music on top of his family's piano.[63] It was a side of him that particularly intrigued Nadia Boulanger, and it put him in touch with the Parisian vogue.

Ragtime music had also figured in a piano arrangement by Igor Stravinsky that was published in 1919, its cover designed by Picasso.[64] For Copland, as for much of Paris, Stravinsky "was the most exciting musical creator on the scene."[65] He met the Russian composer in the early 1920s through Boulanger, whose mother was of Russian origin. Copland must have been impressed, too, when Picasso's three drawings of Stravinsky were reproduced in February 1924 in the first issue of *Modern Music*, the journal of the newly formed League of Composers, of which Copland was a board member.[66]

Picasso produced *Portrait of Igor Stravinsky* in Paris on May 24, 1920, in pencil on gray paper, in his most elegant linear neoclassical style. Picasso and Stravinsky had just collaborated on *Pulcinella*, a new ballet on the commedia dell'arte theme for Serge Diaghilev's Ballets Russes at the Paris Opéra. The change in Picasso's style from cubism inflected by African art to neoclassicism paralleled the dramatic change that Copland had observed in Stravinsky's music in the fall of 1923:

it was a reverse shocker, even after seeing the score at Boulanger's. Its neoclassicism was a curious about-face on Stravinsky's part and indicated a surprising development that nobody could have predicted. Here was Stravinsky—who had created a neoprimitive style that everyone agreed was one of the most original in modern music—now, without any explanation, presenting a piece to the public that bore no resemblance to the style with which he had become identified![67]

Getting Established in New York

A<small>FTER JUST THREE YEARS IN</small> P<small>ARIS</small>, Copland left for New York in June 1924. He later made clear that it was in France that he first grasped "the idea that my personal expression in music ought somehow to be related to my own back-home environment."[68] Although they had previously seemed separate, he now sought to reconcile music and the life around him. About his European experience Copland commented, "It was not so very different from the experience of other young American artists, in other fields, who had gone abroad to study in that period; in greater or lesser degree, all of us discovered America in Europe."[69]

That first autumn back in America Copland finally met the critic Paul Rosenfeld, whose essays on music and art he had been so avidly reading. The occasion was an informal meeting of the League of Composers held at the New York home of its director, Claire Reis. Rosenfeld, who came from a cultivated and affluent German-Jewish background, was to become an important supporter of Copland's, not only through his writing but also by introducing him to the arts patron Alma Morgenthau Wertheim.[70] On Rosenfeld Copland reflected, "Paul was one of the first critics to write perceptively about [Charles] Ives, Ornstein, Varèse, [Carl] Ruggles, [Henry] Cowell, [Roy] Harris, and [Roger] Sessions."[71] He felt moved to add that Rosenfeld "wrote about painting too."[72] Copland also recalled that Rosenfeld's apartment on Irving Place was filled with art and the dinner guests included "the most interesting people in the avant-garde literary, music, and art worlds," naming such figures as Hart Crane, Lewis Mumford, Waldo Frank, E. E. Cummings, and Edmund Wilson.[73]

Copland himself figured in the entertainment for one of Rosenfeld's soirées, as described in a letter by Crane, who saw his own poetry as the pièce de résistance for the occasion (Saturday, November 29, 1924):

The crowd was representative. . . . Steiglitz [sic], Georgia O'Keefe [sic], Seligman, Jean Toomer, Paul Strand and his wife, Alfred Kreymborg, Marianne Moore,

Alfred Stieglitz, Paul Rosenfeld. *Photograph, gelatin silver print, 9 3/16 x 7 5/16" (23.3 x 18.6 cm), 1920. Beinecke Rare Book and Manuscript Library, Yale University, New Haven.*

Van Wyck Brooks, Edmund Wilson and Mary Blair, Lewis Mumford, etc. etc. There was music by Copeland [sic], a modern composer and after that the readings . . .[74]

Wilson recorded a particularly vivid image of Copland among the regulars on the scene *chez* Rosenfeld:

> One met Ornstein, Milhaud, Varèse, Cummings, Hart Crane, and Marianne Moore; the Stieglitzes and all their group; the Stettheimers, Mumford, Kreymborg. One of the images that remains with me most vividly is the bespectacled figure of Copland, at that period gray-faced and lean, long-nosed and rather unearthly, bending over the piano as he chanted in a high, cold, and passionate voice a poem of Ezra Pound's, for which he had written a setting.[75]

Wilson was referring to "An Immorality," which Copland wrote in 1925 to a text by Ezra Pound from *Ripostes* (1912).[76] Copland scored this piece, which begins, "Sing we for love and idleness, Naught else is worth the having," for women's chorus and a piano accompaniment. In it he made deliberate references to jazz.

The influence of jazz is again evident in Copland's *Music for the Theatre*, written during the summer and autumn of 1925 and originally titled *Incidental Music for an Imaginary Drama*. Copland divided his composition into five parts: "Prologue," "Dance," "Interlude," "Burlesque," and "Epilogue." While the first two parts evoke jazz and the third the blues, the fourth refers to the erotic theatricals that flourished in New York during the 1920s and includes a quotation from the popular song "The Sidewalks of New York." Copland explained that his homage to this genre of American popular art was prompted in part by the comedienne Fanny Brice, whose career was launched when she sang Irving Berlin's song "Sadie Salome" with a Yiddish accent.[77] Copland probably saw her perform in

Alvin Langdon Coburn (1882–1966), Ezra Pound. Photograph, collotype print, 7 ¹¹/₁₆ x 6 ¼" (19.5 x 15.8 cm), 1913. National Portrait Gallery, Smithsonian Institution, Washington, D.C.

Reginald Marsh (1898–1954), Burlesk Runway. Etching, state two, 5 x 6 ¾" (12.7 x 17.2 cm), 1927. Print Collection, Miriam and Ira D. Wallach Division of Art, Prints and Photographs, The New York Public Library, Astor, Lenox, and Tilden Foundations, Gift of Felicia Meyer Marsh.

Thomas Hart Benton (1889–1975), Burlesque. Egg tempera on panel, 9 ½ x 12 ½" (24.1 x 31.8 cm), c. 1922. Collection of Edward Suckle.

a burlesque musical comedy such as *Music Box Revue* (1924) or in one of the Ziegfeld Follies.[78]

Copland shared his interest in the motif of burlesque with a number of visual artists. Around 1922 Thomas Hart Benton painted his *Burlesque*, featuring a crowd of portly, balding men staring at the rotating posterior of a female dancer who swirls her red cape like a matador. Elie Nadelman sculpted burlesque strippers in the mid-1920s. Likewise, Reginald Marsh, in *Burlesk Runway* (1927), the first in a series of etchings he made on the subject, depicted female performers as observed by the musicians in the pit, who look up at the scantily attired bodies gyrating above them, even as the patrons focus their gaze from the perspective of their seats.

In burlesque and jazz Copland found means of creating the kind of controversy he had encountered in Ornstein and the Ballets Suédois: "The very idea of jazz in a concert hall was piquant in the twenties," he later wrote, noting that it seemed that "any piece based on jazz was assured of a mild *succès de scandale*."[79] He reflected that jazz "played a big role in the twenties"[80] and later explained, "I was intrigued with jazz rhythms, not for superficial effects, but for use in larger forms, with unconventional harmonies. My aim was to write a work that would be recognizably American within a serious musical idiom. Jazz offered American composers a native product from which to explore rhythm."[81]

When Copland wrote *Music for the Theatre* in 1925, his understanding of jazz was limited to what he had heard of the rapidly developing art by that time. Yet his initial positive response to and continuing appreciation of jazz were nonetheless much greater than what many composers and music critics who were his contemporaries felt.[82] Paul Rosenfeld, for example, argued in 1929 in a book he dedicated to the African-American writer Jean Toomer, "American music is not jazz. Jazz is not music. Jazz remains a striking indigenous product, a small, sounding folk-chaos, counterpart of other national developments."[83]

Rosenfeld would be proven wrong many times over. Jazz has had a major impact. In retrospect, jazz became an emblem for the whole culture of the 1920s, "the jazz age," as F. Scott Fitzgerald described it in an article he wrote for *Scribner's Magazine* in 1931.[84] Writers Copland admired incorporated jazz rhythms in their work, most notably Hart Crane, who in 1922 wrote to a friend, "Let us invent an idiom for the proper transposition of jazz into words! Something clean, sparkling, elusive."[85] Crane's poem "Faustus and Helen" contains rhythms that have been described as approximating jazz dance steps.[86] This may have been among the poems Crane recited at Rosenfeld's home on the evening in 1924 when Copland performed the songs he had set to Pound's poetry.[87] Also in 1924, but on the other side of the Atlantic, the African-American poet Langston Hughes, working in a Paris nightclub featuring jazz, began writing poems influenced by jazz rhythms, including "Jazz Band in a Parisian Cabaret."[88] As late as 1945, William Carlos Williams, a poet who had been closely associated with the Stieglitz circle, wrote "Ol' Bunk's Band," a poem that pays homage to the jagged tempo of black "classical" jazz, just after hearing Bunk Johnson and his New Orleans band play in New York.[89]

The jazz vogue also colored a piece written in 1922 by Copland's friend Carl Van Vechten, who discerned a transfer of musical spirit to the visual arts in the paintings of Florine Stettheimer: "This lady has got into her painting a very modern quality, the quality that ambitious American musicians will have to get in their compositions before any one will listen to them. At the risk of being misunderstood, I must call this quality jazz."[90] He added that "Jazz music, indubitably, is an art in itself, but before a contemporary American can triumph in the serious concert halls he must reproduce not the thing itself but its spirit in a most lasting form."[91] Copland himself satisfied Van Vechten's principle and caught the jazz spirit, to judge from a remark by Clurman that in Copland's work "the jazz itself took on qualities of affectionate irony, sharpness, and acidity that bespoke a slight apartness, a margin of reserve."[92] Copland would continue to be interested in jazz throughout his life, although Clurman identified the mid-twenties as his "jazz period."

Florine Stettheimer and her sisters, Ettie and Carrie, were among the regulars with Copland *chez* Rosenfeld, but they conducted a salon in their

33

Florine Stettheimer (1871–1944), Portrait of Marcel Duchamp. *Oil on canvas, 23 x 23"*
(58.4 x 58.4 cm), c. 1925–1926. Museum of Fine Arts, Springfield, Mass.

*Florine Stettheimer, Portrait of Virgil Thomson. Oil on canvas, 38 ¼ x 20 ⅛"
(97.2 x 51.1 cm), 1930. Art Institute of Chicago, 1975.77.*

New York apartment as well. Located in the Alwyn Court, an ornate building on the corner of Seventh Avenue and Fifty-eighth Street, it was dubbed by Van Vechten "Chateau Stettheimer."[93] The sisters brought diverse interests to their evenings. Ettie was an active feminist and a novelist, while Carrie, who for a time studied music, was known for designing dollhouses, one of which was distinguished by its collection of authentic works of art, produced in miniature for her by Duchamp, Nadelman, and other artists in their circle.[94] By 1929 Copland, Van Vechten, Duchamp, Rosenfeld, O'Keeffe, Stieglitz, Virgil Thomson, Kirk and Constance Askew, and many others in the arts attended the Stettheimers' dinners.[95] Although Florine painted portraits of a number of their guests, including Stieglitz, Van Vechten, Duchamp, and Thomson, she never depicted Copland. One of her portraits of Duchamp (c. 1925–1926) presents just his head, floating saintlike, as if he were in a trance.

By the time Stettheimer painted her *Portrait of Virgil Thomson* in 1930, the two were collaborating on his opera *Four Saints in Three Acts*, with its abstract, plotless libretto by Gertrude Stein. Thomson, who had been incorporating folk songs into his music since the 1920s, created melodies rooted in Anglo-American hymns.[96] Stettheimer designed sets and costumes for the production, which premiered in 1934 at the Wadsworth Atheneum in Hartford, Connecticut, and went on to open on Broadway the next month. When the production, with its all-African-American cast, moved to Chicago, it inspired Stein's friend Francis Strain to make it the subject of a painting, *Four Saints in Three Acts*.

Copland had met Thomson when they were both studying with Boulanger in Paris, but as Copland later recalled, "Virgil was more at home with the French crowd led by Cocteau, who frequented Le Boeuf sur le toit, a bar

35

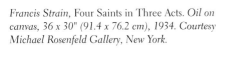

Francis Strain, Four Saints in Three Acts. *Oil on canvas, 36 x 30" (91.4 x 76.2 cm), 1934. Courtesy Michael Rosenfeld Gallery, New York.*

named after a Milhaud score."[97] In 1932 Thomson wrote an article on Copland for *Modern Music*, which he began by announcing, "Aaron Copland's music is American in rhythm, Jewish in melody, eclectic in all the rest."[98] Thomson, who boasted "Nobody . . . is more American than I am," also contended that his work showed Copland "how to treat Americana."[99] Such remarks about who is (or is not) American reflect the racial nativism that flourished around the time (1924) the United States Congress imposed a quota restricting immigration from eastern and southern Europe.[100] This climate allowed the critic Forbes Watson, in his review of the show *Paintings by Nineteen Living Americans* at the new Museum of Modern Art in 1929, to attack the Russian-Jewish émigré Max Weber for "taking no account of the American tradition" and for being tied to "European standards."[101]

Along with George Antheil, both Copland and Thomson (who had made Antheil's acquaintance in Paris in 1923) were among the young American composers who took part in an all-American concert arranged by Boulanger in Paris in the spring of 1926. For Copland, this concert was an excuse to return to Paris. Traveling with Clurman, he stayed in Europe five months, also briefly visiting Germany, where, in Munich, the two felt frightened by what Clurman later characterized as "the rising Nazi movement."[102]

In Paris Copland attended the premiere on June 19, 1926, of Antheil's *Ballet Mécanique*, described as performed by a "reduced" orchestra and retitled "Ballet pour Instruments mécaniques et percussion." Antheil had intended a

motion-picture accompaniment for his piece, but coordinating the score with the abstract film of objects in motion and rhythmic patterns meant to synchronize with the beat of the music was difficult, until he eventually cut and simplified his music. Directed by Fernand Léger in collaboration with the American cameraman Dudley Murphy, the film was originally supposed to accompany music produced by seventeen player pianos, airplane propellers, and kettledrums.[103]

Describing the Paris premiere in a letter to a friend, Copland named some of the notables in the "audience of more than 2,000 people" who bore special interest for him, among them Pound, Milhaud, and Duchamp.[104] For the New York premiere of *Ballet Mécanique* in April 1927, Antheil invited Copland to be one of ten pianists onstage at Carnegie Hall.[105]

Miguel Covarrubias (1904–1957), George Antheil. Drawing published in the New York Sun, *April 9, 1927.*

Charles Demuth, Longhi on Broadway. *Oil on board, 33 ⅞ x 27" (86 x 68.6 cm), 1928. Museum of Fine Arts, Boston, Gift of the William Lane Foundation, 1990.397.*

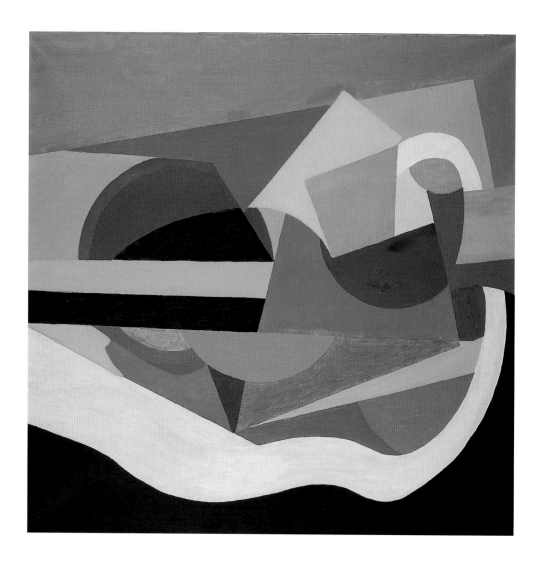

e. e. cummings (1894–1962), Sound. Oil on canvas, 35 x 35 ⅛" (88.9 x 89.2 cm), 1919. Metropolitan Museum of Art, New York, Bequest of Scofield Thayer, 1982, 1984.433.8.

The American performance, however, was poorly received and also omitted the film. The two pieces were not performed together until October 18, 1935, at the Museum of Modern Art in New York, with the music arranged for just one pianola.

Writing two years earlier for *Modern Music*, Copland had called Antheil "a talented young American composer" who had toured Germany as "a self-styled futurist composer" and published "wild manifestoes in the avant-garde magazines."[106] This was, however, not enough emphasis for Antheil, who wrote to the magazine to complain: "My concerts in Europe have not 'resembled' riots—they were riots."[107] Pound, too, wrote about Antheil, stressing his American qualities. Both Man Ray and his assistant, Berenice Abbott, photographed him. Demuth referred to Antheil in his canvas *Longhi on Broadway* of 1928, a still life featuring a group of magazines, including a special issue of *This Quarter* devoted to Antheil, his name prominently visible on its cover.[108]

Copland's awareness of Antheil's deep interest in the visual arts is evident from their correspondence. In 1933, Antheil wrote to Copland telling him that his friend the surrealist Joan Miró was trying "to jazz up Barcelona" by organizing some sort of modern society.[109] A few months later he told Copland that among the pieces he wanted to play at the Festival of Contemporary Music at the artists' colony Yaddo were his "100 piano preludes to Femme Cent Tete of Max Ernst's" and his *Sonatina*, which was dedicated to Copland, "in admiration of your work, and in appreciation of your friendship."[110] Antheil clearly qualified for the ranks of modernists provoking controversy, who, as we have seen, ever appealed to Copland.

Another provocative modernist who engaged Copland's attention was the poet-painter E. E. Cummings, whose work the composer first encountered in *The Dial* and whom he met at one of Rosenfeld's soirées. In 1927, exploring advanced idioms, Copland scored one of Cummings's poems for voice and piano, resulting in *Song*. The ten-line poem, from the collection entitled *is 5*, published the previous year, begins with the words "in spite of everything" and describes, according to Cummings, "precision that creates movement."[111] Cummings not only wrote and painted works aimed at vanguard audiences, but played the piano and understood musical notation and composition as well.[112] His paintings, which show him immersed in the esthetics of abstraction, won him recognition before his writing did. Cummings had felt the influence of the Italian futurists and the cubist Gleizes; in *Sound* of 1919 he explored making sound visible and, at the same time, suggested the form of a guitar.[113] He and Copland shared an enthusiasm for Stravinsky, whose *Petroushka* had made quite an impression on Cummings in 1917 in Paris.[114]

39

Explorations of Folk Idioms

STRAVINSKY HAD CAUGHT COPLAND'S EAR during those first years in Paris, for reasons that reveal his own musical agenda: "This extraordinary rhythmic puissance Stravinsky owes to his Russian heritage—to the folk songs of his country."[115] Copland recalled that Stravinsky "borrowed freely from folk materials, and I have no doubt that this strongly influenced me to try to find a way to a distinctively American music."[116]

Mexican and Native American Themes   Copland's interest in folk music may have encouraged him to forge cultural links with Mexico. Through his mentor and friend Paul Rosenfeld, he met the Mexican composer Carlos Chávez, whom Rosenfeld praised in his book *By Way of Art* (1928) for the "original aspects of his work," which "make us feel America," extolling "his passion for the relics of Aztec culture as well as the forms of existing life."[117] The essay was juxtaposed with one about Copland.[118] The very next year, in a book called *An Hour with American Music*, Rosenfeld once again devoted adjacent essays to Copland and Chávez. The work of Chávez, he reiterated, was "manifestly un-European," and Rosenfeld emphasized his connection "with the American soil and the savage chants of the Indians. Himself part amerindian, the atonal sing-song of his lyrical themes strongly recalls the crowing and cackling of the red-man in his dusty pueblos."[119] Thanks to Rosenfeld, the two composers became friends. In a letter to Copland in 1930 Chávez inquired about Rosenfeld, saying that he often thought about the critic and asking to be remembered to him.[120] Copland, writing from Saratoga Springs, New York, replied that Rosenfeld was spending the summer with Stieglitz at Lake George and that he would soon see him and bring news of Chávez.[121]

Copland recalled meeting Chávez for the first time not long after the latter's arrival in New York from Mexico in the fall of 1926.[122] Chávez was then living in a tenement on Fourteenth Street, where he roomed with the painter Rufino Tamayo. The sociable young Mexicans met their neighbors and made new friends, including the artists Stuart Davis, Reginald Marsh, Yasuo Kuniyoshi, and Duchamp.[123] Although in New York, both Chávez and Tamayo maintained their interest in indigenous Indian culture and their sympathy for the Mexican Revolution, and for ensuing art initiatives by the new government.

Tamayo's interest in music is evident in his woodcuts *Guitar Player* and *Mermaids* (both c. 1926–1930), as well as in his paintings *Mandolins and Pineapples* (1930) and *Los Musicos* (1934). In the latter canvas, Tamayo painted three guitarists with faces of different colors, perhaps signifying racial harmony between the indigenous peoples and other cultures. In fact, he played

Rufino Tamayo (1899–1991),
Guitar Player. *Woodcut on paper,*
6 11/16 x 5 1/8" (17 x 13 cm),
c. 1926–1930. Metropolitan
Museum of Art, New York, Gift
of Jean Charlot, 1931, 31.91.29.

Rufino Tamayo, Mermaids. *Woodcut on paper, 6 1/8 x 8 1/4" (15.6 x 21 cm), c. 1926–1930.*
Metropolitan Museum of Art, New York, Gift of Jean Charlot, 1931, 31.91.30.

the guitar and sang Mexican folk songs about the ideals and program of Mexican government reform.[124] Musical recitals in New York featured songs by Chávez performed by Lupe Medina, with Tamayo on the guitar. At some of these events, the artist and illustrator Miguel Covarrubias, who collected folk art, presented his *corridos*, emotional songs similar to American country & western ballads.[125] Covarrubias also forged ties with the world of avant-garde American composers, becoming a friend of George Antheil, whom he would caricature (p. 36).[126]

The enthusiasm of Copland's Mexican friends for indigenous folk songs and folk art fueled his own investigations into folk music and ethnic identity. Writing about Chávez in 1928, Copland cited the composer's "use of folk material in its relation to nationalism" as a major trait of modern music.[127] He spent May and June of 1928 in Santa Fe, New Mexico, where no visitor could ignore the presence of picturesque adobe houses and active Spanish folk traditions, which included Spanish-American folk songs, some of them "imported from Old Mexico."[128] While in Santa Fe, Copland hired two young artists, Charles (Chuck) Barrows and James S. Morris, to drive him to Taos, another artists' colony.[129] The two young men had come to Santa Fe under the influence of the painter John Sloan, who had a strong interest in the Native American culture of the area. At the time, Copland was en route to California, where in July he was to play his *Piano Concerto* at the Hollywood Bowl, but he decided to visit New

Rufino Tamayo, Los Musicos (The Musicians). *Oil on canvas, 1934. Private collection.*

Rufino Tamayo, Self-Portrait. Gouache on paper, 9 ¹⁵/₁₆ x 7"
(25.2 x 17.7 cm), 1927. Cleveland Museum of Art, Gift of Mrs. Malcolm L. McBride, 1957.

Mexico on the way, recalling, "I had heard about Santa Fe from artist and writer friends who told me I could find an inexpensive room with a piano there"[130] and admitting to Boulanger, "I suppose it is time for me to see America a little."[131]

Jewish Themes   Copland spent much of his two months in Santa Fe working on *Vitebsk*, a "Study on a Jewish Theme for violin, 'cello, & piano," which drew on the ethnic roots of his family. First the composer Roger Sessions, then Virgil Thomson had written about the Jewish elements in Copland's music.[132] He later explained, "I grew up in the Eastern European tradition" but "It was always a musical stimulus that got me started, as when I heard the folk theme that the Polish-Jewish author S. Ansky used in his play *The Dybbuk*.[133] It appealed to me just as it had to him. Vitebsk, a small Russian village, was the playwright's home."[134]

Copland subsequently described the fast section of *Vitebsk* as "a Chagall-like grotesquerie that reaches a wild climax and interrupts itself in mid-course, causing a dramatic pause."[135] In the period when he was composing *Vitebsk*, the paintings by Chagall immortalizing the town were becoming better known. Harold Clurman recalled that he was attracted to Chagall's work in 1922, when he and Copland were constant companions in Paris.[136] A 1928 monograph on Chagall reproduced the theatrical picture *Green Violinist* (1923–1924).[137]

Scene from The Dybbuk, Habimah Theatre *production, c. 1926. Anonymous photograph, gelatin silver print, 13 x 10 ¼" (33 x 26 cm), c. 1964. The New York Public Library for the Performing Arts, Billy Rose Theatre Collection.*

45

Marc Chagall (1887–1985), Green Violinist (Violoniste). Oil on canvas, 77 x 42 ½" (195.6 x 108 cm), 1923–1924. Solomon R. Guggenheim Museum, New York, Gift of Solomon R. Guggenheim, 1937, 37.446. © Artists Rights Society (ARS), New York/ADAGP, Paris.

Whether or not Copland saw this painting or a reproduction of it while working on *Vitebsk*, the image expresses in visual terms the energetic spirit of folk music in village life. Chagall conceived of this violinist as the personification of music, indeed, as representing all of the arts available to Russian villagers, who had no orchestras, no museums, and no paintings. Chagall's uncle in Vitebsk played the violin and taught his nephew the instrument, so it should not surprise us that images of violinists recur in Chagall's work.[138] The music Chagall heard and played was surely similar to the folk tune that Copland borrowed for *Vitebsk*.

American Folk Art   The vogue of folk art and culture was captivating artists in many countries and media. Marsden Hartley, whose work Copland would have seen at Stieglitz's gallery, at Rosenfeld's, and elsewhere, had investigated folk paintings on glass in both Germany (where the tradition was known as *Hinterglasmalerei*) and Maine during the 1910s.[139] In 1924 the Whitney Studio Club held an exhibition titled *Early American Art*, to which several contemporary artists lent folk art they had collected, including Kuniyoshi, whom Copland came to know.[140]

In 1926 the émigré sculptor Elie Nadelman and his wife founded their Museum of Folk Arts to show their vast collections from both Europe and America, including several decorated American rooms. They emphasized popular crafts in America together with examples of their European sources. Extant photographs document one "All-American" room that featured braced-back Windsor chairs and a child's Windsor chair, a hutch table, a pottery milk bowl, "primitive" paintings on velvet, and an early nineteenth-century embroidery. Another "American Corner" in the museum displayed a patchwork quilt, a hooked rug, a doll, a child's rocking chair, and a cradle.

Nadelman's own art sometimes simultaneously reflected his interest in folk traditions and music. For example, in about 1918, he sculpted such figures as *Woman at the Piano, Cellist, Chanteuse*, and *The Orchestra Conductor* in both plaster (now destroyed) and wood. These were all themes that later appealed to ballet impresario Lincoln Kirstein, who became one of the artist's most ardent promoters. Kirstein, who compared Nadelman to Stravinsky, eventually owned a large collection of Nadelman's work, including his folk art–inspired drawing *Top-Hatted Man with Borzoi Dog* (c. 1916–1920).[141] In 1948, he arranged a posthumous show of Nadelman's work at the Museum of Modern Art.[142]

American folk art was linked to modernism in New York by Edith Gregor Halpert, who added it to her Downtown Gallery in 1929 (and in 1933 had her inventory of folk art photographed by Walker Evans). Also in 1929, Copland's *Vitebsk* was performed for the first time; and Edward Hopper purchased an anonymous folk painting, the only work of art of the past he ever bought.[143] In 1932, New York's Museum of Modern Art presented a show entitled *American Folk Art: The Art of the Common Man in America, 1750–1900*, organized by the folklorist and curator Holger Cahill.

It was in 1932, coinciding with Cahill's show, that Carl Van Vechten photographed Copland's distinctive profile against sheet music (p. 120) and again in front of a patchwork quilt (p. 50). Quilts—homemade and hand sewn— evoked rustic Americana, pioneer virtues of thrift and ingenuity.[144] Households from Colonial times through the mid-nineteenth century routinely produced and used quilts. Van Vechten had clearly heard Copland's call for an American music, and as Copland would later recall, "The desire to be 'American' was symptomatic of the period."[145]

"All-American" interior (top) and "American Corner" (below) at the Museum of Folk Arts, Riverdale-on-Hudson, New York, founded by Elie Nadelman in 1926. Anonymous photographs, n.d. Collection of the Nadelman Family.

Copland and Van Vechten's interest in folk music and culture was shared by Thomas Hart Benton, as evidenced by his canvas *Missouri Musicians* of 1931 (p. 51), which depicts three men seated outdoors playing an accordion, a guitar, and a fiddle. Benton had traveled to Galena, Missouri, to hear country music by the famous Leverett Brothers in the summer of 1931, and he used his sketches of them for this painting.[146] The next year, Benton included a similar vignette of three folk musicians in *Arts of the West*, one of his series of murals called The Arts of Life in America painted for the library of New York's Whitney Museum.[147] Benton recalled that he always searched for musicians in his travels around the country, and noted, "I've played with, and for, the hill folks on a harmonica and have picked up unwritten tunes and odd variants of those which have found their way into music books."[148] Tom and Rita Benton's loft on Eighth Street in Manhattan was the scene of many "Saturday nights," when musician friends such as Ruth Crawford and Charles Seeger, Carl Ruggles, and Henry Cowell gathered to sing folk songs.[149]

In January 1931 Seeger performed with a small pickup band of singers at a party held at the New School for Social Research to celebrate Benton's completion of another cycle of murals, America Today, one of which, *City Activities with Subway*, features burlesque dancers in the upper left corner. Copland had been arranging concerts and teaching at the New School since 1927, a position he inherited from his friend Paul Rosenfeld.[150] Thus, surely Copland became aware that Rosenfeld detested Benton's work. Rosenfeld attacked Benton and his Whitney Museum murals in a 1933 article, writing that "the arts of life in America are thoroughly crude, gross and ungracious."[151] Ironically, Benton's

Elie Nadelman (1882–1946), left to right: Cellist; The Orchestra Conductor; Woman at the Piano. *Plaster, 1918 (all destroyed). Photographs by Mattie Edwards Hewitt, n.d. Collection of the Nadelman Family.*

Arts of the West was chosen as the cover illustration for the booklet of a 1994 compact disk of Copland's music.[152]

Benton became widely identified as a Regionalist artist from 1934, when *Time* magazine featured him on its cover as a leading painter of the American scene.[153] The identification of Benton, Grant Wood, and John Steuart Curry as a Midwestern triumvirate evoked harsh criticism in New York, as did Benton's vociferous pronouncements against the left. Although in the early twenties Benton had been a Marxist who voted for the Socialist ticket, by the end of the decade he had become disenchanted with orthodox Marxism.[154] The writing of one of Benton's biggest supporters, one-time *Dial* art critic Thomas Craven, began to reveal that his own search for national identity in art was linked to xenophobia and prejudice, further alienating progressive thinkers such as Rosenfeld, who had been his colleague at *The Dial*.[155]

49

Elie Nadelman, Top-Hatted Man with Borzoi Dog. Pencil and ink on paper, 9 ⅜ x 8" (23.8 x 20.3 cm), c. 1916–1920. Private collection, New York.

50

Carl Van Vechten (1880–1964), Aaron Copland. *Photograph, gelatin silver print, 7 x 5" (17.8 x 12.7 cm), 1932. Copland Collection, Library of Congress, Washington, D.C.* © *Carl Van Vechten Trust.*

Thomas Hart Benton, City Activities with Subway *(from* America Today *mural cycle). Distemper and egg tempera with oil glaze on gessoed linen, 92 x 134 ½" (233.7 x 341.6 cm), 1930. Collection of AXA Financial, through its subsidiary The Equitable Life Assurance Society of the U.S. © AXA Financial.*

Thomas Hart Benton, Arts of the West *(1932), as reproduced on cover of CD brochure for Leonard Slatkin, dir.,* Copland: Music for Films, *Saint Louis Symphony Orchestra, BMG/RCA Victor 61699, 1994.*

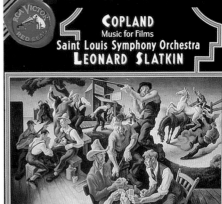

Thomas Hart Benton, Missouri Musicians. Tempera *on canvas, 29 x 34 ¾"
(73.7 x 88.3 cm), 1931. Collection of Ruth and Abraham Feingold.*

Contested Cultural Leadership

THIS MOMENT MARKED A PARTICULARLY VICIOUS STRUGGLE over who would control the search for an American national culture—the avant-garde, experimental strain represented by Rosenfeld, Waldo Frank, and Stieglitz, or a more conservative group of artists and critics that included Benton and Craven. Following Rosenfeld's attack on Benton's murals, which Benton dismissed as part of "a new storm of left-wing criticism of my work," the artist wrote a nasty review of a volume called *America and Alfred Stieglitz*, edited by Frank, Lewis Mumford, Rosenfeld, Dorothy Norman, and Harold Rugg and published in honor of Stieglitz's seventieth birthday.[156] Calling his review "America and/or Alfred Stieglitz," Benton attacked what he identified as "the mental character of a group of intellectuals who keep themselves in the public prints."[157]

Yet despite their differences, the two camps shared some important interests. All were striving to define a national identity for America, in part through emphasizing its folk culture. This approach had attracted such diverse figures as Benton and Copland, as well as Hartley and other artists squarely in the Stieglitz circle such as Paul Strand and Arthur G. Dove. While Alfred Stieglitz had shown a mix of European and American works in his first gallery (291), by 1925, when he opened The Intimate Gallery, he showed only American artists.

Alfred Stieglitz, Songs of the Sky. *Photograph, gelatin silver print, 3 ¾ x 4 ⅝" (9.5 x 11.8 cm), 1924. The Phillips Collection, Washington, D.C., Alfred Stieglitz Collection, Gift of Georgia O'Keeffe, 1949.*

In addition to his own photographs, Stieglitz emphasized work by O'Keeffe, Marin, Hartley, Demuth, Dove, and Strand. Reflecting this emphasis on art produced by Americans, his last gallery, which opened in December 1929, was called An American Place.

Describing An American Place, the photographer and writer Dorothy Norman, who was Stieglitz's last companion, mentions, in addition to the artists who showed there, some of the people who frequented the gallery, including "the composers Edgar [sic] Varèse, Ernest Bloch or Aaron Copland."[158] Among others she noted are many who figured importantly for Copland: Hart Crane, E. E. Cummings, Carl Van Vechten, Paul Rosenfeld, and the Stettheimer sisters, as well as Harold Clurman and Clifford Odets, who are identified as members of the emergent Group Theatre (for which Copland, Stieglitz, and Norman all served as board members). In the period when Clurman recalled that he, Copland, and the writer Gerald Sykes were inseparable, he remembered visiting the gallery and listening to Stieglitz talk for hours about painting.[159] Copland himself recalled how he knew that Stieglitz would give "a sympathetic ear" to anything new in the arts.[160]

53

Stieglitz's dual interests in music and modernism are reflected in his photographs of the 1920s, some of which are known as Equivalents. Using titles such as *Music: A Sequence of Ten Cloud Photographs* (1922) and *Songs of the Sky* (1923 and 1924), Stieglitz, whose earliest tastes in music were Germanic (Mozart, Beethoven, Bruckner, Brahms, and Johann Strauss), sought to create visual music, treating nature increasingly abstractly.[161] He explained that he wanted to make photographs that would cause his friend Ernest Bloch to exclaim, "Music! Music! Man, why that is music! How did you ever do that?"[162] A Swiss-born Jewish immigrant, Bloch, too, aspired to create an American culture, winning a contest in 1927 with his rhapsody for chorus and orchestra entitled *America*. Copland himself had been an enthusiast of Bloch's work, so much so that during his student days in Paris he had written to his parents requesting that they send him his sheet music of songs by Bloch.[163] A few months later, he implored them to purchase and send him Bloch's *Suite for Viola and Piano.*[164]

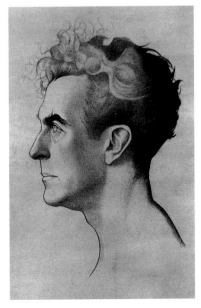

Joseph Stella (1877–1946), Portrait of Edgar Varèse. *Silverpoint on paper, 22 x 16" (55.9 x 40.6 cm), c. 1922. Baltimore Museum of Art, Special Fund for the Purchase of Art, BMA, 1963.114.*

Copland recalled that it was at Stieglitz's gallery in the late 1920s that he met "the salty New Englander" Carl Ruggles, who though a generation older than he, was esteemed by the avant-garde in New York.[165] Not only a composer, Ruggles also painted. Yet the visual artists who were his friends—Benton, Rockwell Kent, and Boardman Robinson—were distinct from those in Copland's circle. Moreover, Copland, whose music had been presented in New York by the League of Composers, could not be allied with that organization's rival, the International Composers' Guild, to which Ruggles and Edgard Varèse belonged. (The League had been founded in 1923 by four Guild members who had had a falling out with Varèse.) During the 1920s, both Ruggles and Varèse received the support of Gertrude Vanderbilt Whitney, the socialite sculptor who founded the Whitney Studio Club, which, by 1931, had evolved into the Whitney Museum of American Art.[166]

Despite Ruggles's infamous "New England prejudices," the open-minded Copland admired his music and included Ruggles's *Portals* in a concert of modern American music he produced in Berlin on December 9, 1931; years later, when he began conducting, he chose the piece for his programs.[167] What is remarkable is that Ruggles, who in the late 1920s cursed out "god-damned Ellis Islanders" and challenged the right of composers of non-British descent to call themselves "American," also frequented Stieglitz's gallery.[168] Although

he eventually bought into the growing fear of foreigners and radicals that followed World War I, at the time Ruggles arrived in New York, in August 1917, he cultivated Socialists as friends, including Kent and Robinson. These contacts enabled him to conduct the Workers Symphony Orchestra at The Rand School for Social Science, an institution dedicated to workers' education operated by the American Socialist Society.[169] Marxist ideas must have once held an appeal for him, because his name is listed among the editorial staff of *New Masses* in its first year's worth of issues (1926), although not thereafter.[170]

Thomas Hart Benton, "The Sun Treader" (Portrait of Carl Ruggles). Oil on canvas, 45 x 38" (114.3 x 96.5 cm), 1934. Nelson-Atkins Museum of Art, Kansas City, Mo.

By the time Benton painted Ruggles's portrait, both men had moved to the right politically. *"The Sun Treader"—Portrait of Carl Ruggles* (1934) refers to the composer's most famous composition, named after a line from "Pauline," Robert Browning's 1833 elegy to Percy Bysshe Shelley: "Sun-Treader, life and light be thine forever." Benton's friendship with Ruggles dated from the mid-1920s, when he, Varèse, Seeger, Thomas Craven, and others frequently gathered at soirées held at the New York home of Tom and Sarah Kelly, a wealthy couple from Philadelphia.[171] Pleased with the portrait, Benton wrote to Ruggles, commenting that although "Charlie [Seeger] says (in fun) that the piano looks like it's going to take flight . . . it's the best thing I've done this winter."[172]

The Search for an American Art

COPLAND SHARED WITH MANY of the artists and others in the Stieglitz circle the ambition to make "American" art. Both he and Georgia O'Keeffe, for example, responded to Waldo Frank's complaint of 1919 that "America is a turmoiled giant who cannot speak . . . his tongue is tied."[173] Rosenfeld had written about American painting in *The Dial*, calling for works that "speak to the American of what lies between him and his native soil."[174] But the talk of creating an American culture also extended well beyond the Stieglitz circle.

55

Georgia O'Keeffe (1887–1986), Evening Star No. 2. Watercolor on paper,
9 x 19" (22.9 x 48.3 cm), 1917. Private collection.

56

Arthur Dove (1880–1946), George Gershwin—Rhapsody in Blue, Part II. Oil on metal, 20 ½ x 15 ½" (52.1 x 39.4 cm), 1927. Collection of Michael Scharf.

Edward Hopper reflected such sentiments in an article he wrote in 1927: "We should not be quite certain of the crystallization of the art of America into something native and distinct, were it not that our drama, our literature and our architecture show very evident signs of doing just that thing."[175]

Self-conscious of the need for American subject matter, O'Keeffe moved away from the abstraction that characterized her work during the late 1910s (*Evening Star No. 2* of 1917, for example) and painted such "Native" American

57

Arthur Dove, Swing Music (Louis Armstrong). *Oil on canvas, 17 ⅝ x 25 ⅞" (44.8 x 65.7 cm), 1938. Art Institute of Chicago, Gift of Georgia O'Keeffe from the estate of Alfred Stieglitz.*

images as a Hopi kachina doll (1936) and such emblematic New York images as *Radiator Building—Night, New York* (1927) and *Brooklyn Bridge* (1948). The intention to create a national icon was certainly on her mind when she painted her canvas *Cow's Skull—Red, White and Blue* in 1931, featuring a cow's skull, so evocative of the American Southwest, and the colors of the American flag. Mindful of critics' nationalism, she remarked of her "American painting," "They will not think it great, with the red stripes down the sides—Red, White, and Blue—but they will notice."[176] Ironically, O'Keeffe, who played the violin and painted several abstractions she entitled "music," failed to comprehend Copland's music (despite its celebrated Americanness), as she admitted to him in a 1968 letter she wrote in response to his gift to her of recordings of some of his work: "It has always annoyed me that your music does not speak to me— I always enjoy seeing you . . ."[177]

Paul Strand (1890–1976), Man, Tenancingo de Degollado, Mexico. Photograph, gelatin silver print, 9 3/16 x 7 1/4" (23.3 x 18.4 cm), 1933. Collection of Center for Creative Photography, University of Arizona, Tucson. © 1940 Aperture Foundation, Inc., Paul Strand Archive.

Among the artists in Stieglitz's gallery, Arthur Dove seemed especially sympathetic to contemporary music.[178] During the twenties, he painted several works in homage to the music of George Gershwin, such as *George Gershwin— Rhapsody in Blue, Part I* and *Part II* (p. 56), and *I'll Build a Stairway to Paradise— Gershwin*, all of 1927.[179] Copland commented about Gershwin, who, like himself, had responded to jazz: "In many ways Gershwin and I had much in common— both from Brooklyn, we had studied with Rubin Goldmark [Copland's first composition teacher] during the same time and were pianists and composers of music that incorporated indigenous American sounds . . . but until the Hollywood years in the thirties, we moved in very different circles."[180] Enthusiastic about jazz,

Paul Strand, Carlos Chávez. *Photograph, 6 x 7" (15.2 x 17.8 cm), 1931. Herbert Weinstock Collection, Music Division, The New York Public Library for the Performing Arts, Astor, Lenox, and Tilden Foundations. © 1976 Aperture Foundation, Inc., Paul Strand Archive.*

59

Dove made an abstract painting titled *Swing Music (Louis Armstrong)* in 1938 (p. 57). Copland, who, by the late 1930s especially liked the music of Duke Ellington, discussed Armstrong in a 1958 interview in which he allowed that he wished he could take a month off and listen to the latest jazz.[181]

Of all the artists in the Stieglitz circle, Copland was closest to the photographer Paul Strand, whom he met about 1927. Strand, who was ten years older than Copland, shared his political views. Both men were close friends and supporters of Harold Clurman, who in 1931 became a cofounder of the Group Theatre, created to present socially relevant American plays at affordable prices. During the 1930s Copland and Strand spent time working in Mexico. Strand's photograph *Man, Tenancingo de Degollado, Mexico* of 1933 exemplifies what Copland praised as "the sense of human warmth" in Strand's work.[182]

Strand concurred with Copland's enthusiasm for Mexico and Carlos Chávez, whom he photographed. Copland recalled, "Chávez and I admired each other's music."[183] The first performance of Chávez's orchestral music outside Mexico took place at New York's Aeolian Hall on November 28, 1926, and Copland was probably in attendance, as he and Chávez had become acquainted that fall. The concert presented music for "La Danza de los Hombres y las Máquinas" ("The Dance of the Men and the Machines"), a piece that was subsequently incorporated into Chávez's ballet of 1932, *Horsepower (H.P.)*.

Chávez began collaborating on *H.P.* with the great Mexican muralist Diego Rivera in the late 1920s, with Rivera designing the sets and costumes. (It was probably through Chávez that Copland met Rivera.) Paul Rosenfeld compared the two Mexicans in a book: "Indeed, Chávez's music like Rivera's painting thrills us with the prospect of the great role Mexico may play in the development of an American culture."[184] Chávez described the ballet, which contrasts the machine age of the industrial North with the traditional Mexican agrarian life it affected, as "a symphony of sounds around us, a revue of our times."[185] Copland, for his part, commented that "the symbolic machine-age music at the end of his ballet" reflected "many of the usual modern trends."[186]

Although *H.P.* was described as using "primitive Indian" and Aztec folk music, its four scenes were said to lack a plot. However, the *New York Times* reviewer noted that Rivera's decor and costumes were "alive with comment."[187] After the ballet, Rivera produced an album of the colorful costumes he had designed for such figures as the man, H.P., danced by Alexis Dolinoff, and The Siren, danced by Dorothie Littlefield. (Abby Aldrich Rockefeller purchased this album and later donated it to the Museum of Modern Art.)[188]

Chávez came to the United States for the third time in 1932, staying from February to April.[189] During this time Leopold Stokowski conducted *Horsepower*, which premiered in Philadelphia on March 31, 1932; Copland may have been present at the ballet's opening. It was then that Chávez persuaded Copland to travel to Mexico City for the occasion of an all-Copland program, the first ever given anywhere, which Chávez conducted on September 2, 1932.

Diego Rivera (1886–1957), No. 8. Siren. Costume design for the ballet H.P. *(Horse Power). Watercolor and pencil on paper, 14 x 10" (35.8 x 25.6 cm), 1927. Museum of Modern Art, New York, Gift of Abby Aldrich Rockefeller, 505.41.1.*

Diego Rivera, The Man. Costume design for the ballet H.P. *(Horse Power). Watercolor and pencil on paper, 20 2/3 x 29" (53 x 74.6 cm). Museum of Modern Art, New York, Gift of Abby Aldrich Rockefeller, 505.41.1.*

Mexico

SUCH WAS THE ALLURE OF THE FOLK MUSIC Copland heard in Mexico
that he went on to compose *El Salón México* (1932–1936). He later ascribed
the inspiration for the piece to a memorable experience he had had on his
first trip to Mexico: "When Chávez took me to an unusual night spot called El
Salón México, the atmosphere of this dance hall impressed me, and I came away
with the germ of a musical idea."[190] Years later the young singer Jimmy Turpin
sent him a watercolor caricature by Ruth Keahey entitled *El Saloon Mexico*
(1944), showing Copland in a Mexican saloon playing a piano while a cat
appears to dance across its top. In the distance we see more of Copland's
audience: a man seated at the bar wearing a wide sombrero and a red serape;
a cowboy dressed in boots, hat, and holster standing to his right, near a
brass spittoon; and a bartender sporting a handlebar moustache. Copland
remembered his experience in an article titled "The Story Behind 'El
Salón México,'" illustrated by photographs of Mexican musicians taken by
his young companion at the time, Victor Kraft. In the same article, he wrote
that he had first learned of El Salón México in art critic Anita Brenner's
guidebook on Mexico; she described a "Harlem type night-club for the peepul,
grand Cuban orchestra, Salón México."[191]

    Mexican folk music, which Copland had first heard in New York during
Chávez and Rufino Tamayo's stay there in the mid- to late 1920s, had the appeal
of popular accessibility, which would become an important ideal for the

61

Ruth Keahey, El Saloon
Mexico. *Watercolor on
paper, 6 x 8" (15.2 x 20.3
cm), 1944. Copland
Collection, Library of
Congress, Washington,
D.C.*

political left. (Tamayo returned to New York in 1936 as part of the Mexican Delegation of the left-wing Artists' Congress.) One of Copland's sources for *El Salón México* was *Cancionero Mexicano,* a collection of Mexican folk songs illustrated by Tamayo and published in book form in 1931 by the American anthropologist Frances Toor. In Mexico City in 1932, Toor gave Copland a copy of the book, which meant so much to him that he presented it to the Library of Congress in 1957 along with his manuscript for *El Salón México.* In meeting Toor, Copland had found the leading source on Mexican folk culture. From 1925 through 1937 she published a bilingual magazine called *Mexican Folkways,* which stressed the value of Mexico's folk art and traditional culture. Among those who worked with her or contributed material were Diego Rivera, Rufino Tamayo, Jean Charlot, and Tina Modotti.[192]

Reflecting upon his stay in Mexico, Copland wrote to his friend Mary Lescaze, "Europe now seems conventional to me by comparison. Mexico offers something fresh and pure and wholesome—a quality which is deeply unconventionalized."[193]

During Copland's 1932 Mexican sojourn, Chávez had arranged for the Ministry of Education in Mexico City to display a show of photographs by Paul Strand.[194] On hand to help hang the show there happened to be another close

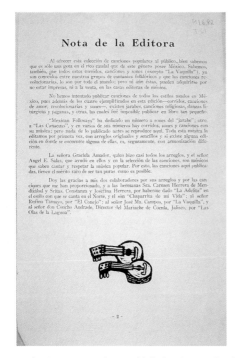

Rufino Tamayo, woodcuts published in Frances Toor's Cancionero Mexicano, 1931.

friend of Strand's, Marsden Hartley, who was in Mexico on a Guggenheim fellowship. Copland probably first came across Hartley's work in reading *The Seven Arts*, to which Hartley had contributed articles in 1917.[195] Copland's friend the artist Richard Hennessy recalls that the composer owned a photograph of Hartley, a painter, poet, and essayist who showed with Stieglitz. In 1932 Hartley was painting intensely colored views of the Mexican landscape, such as *Carnelian Country*, influenced by his reading of mystical texts.[196]

Hartley was but one of a number of homosexual American expatriates in Mexico in 1932, which included the artist Mark Tobey and Copland's old acquaintance Hart Crane. Crane's suicide at sea that year on his way back to New York prompted Hartley to make a commemorative painting, *Eight Bells Folly: Memorial to Hart Crane*, finished in 1933. Copland, too, thought of making a memorial to the dead poet, sketching a page in his notebook with the heading "Elegy for Hart Crane."[197] Both Copland and Hartley were friends of Gertrude Stein, although Hartley, the elder of the two men, had met her as early as 1912. Hartley and Copland did not, however, become close, despite their mutual friends and sexual preference. Rather than Copland's music, Hartley preferred that of earlier composers such as Bach, on whose work he had based some abstract paintings during the 1910s. Although he admired Native American

63

Marsden Hartley (1877–1943), Carnelian Country. Oil on cardboard, 23 ⅞ x 28 ¾" (60.6 x 73 cm), 1932. The Regis Collection, Minneapolis.

dancing and "Negro syncopation," there is no evidence to suggest that he enjoyed the work of contemporary classical composers such as Copland.[198]

Many of Gertrude Stein's friendships overlapped with Copland's; among the friends they had in common were Carl Van Vechten, George Antheil, Virgil Thomson, and Paul Bowles. Stein and her companion Alice B. Toklas had welcomed Bowles (then still a composer and only later a writer) and Copland in the spring of 1931 to spend a weekend with them at Stein's country home near Grenoble, France. Stein recalled in *The Autobiography of Alice B. Toklas* that "Aaron Copeland [sic] came to see us with Bowles in the summer and Gertrude Stein liked him immensely. Bowles told Gertrude Stein and it pleased her that Copeland [sic] said threateningly to him when as usual in the winter he was neither delightful nor sensible, if you do not work now when you are twenty when you are thirty, nobody will love you."[199]

64

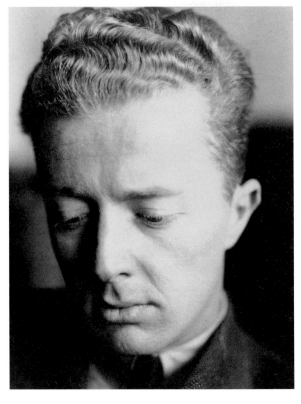

Political Engagement

AFTER ALSO SPENDING TIME IN TANGIER and Berlin during his European stay of 1931, Copland returned to the United States, where the Depression had energized and given focus to longings for change. Back in New York he became more involved in politics, specifically that of the left wing. Without abandoning modernism, he began to examine folk culture while remaining unafraid of controversy and innovation. Copland had shown leftist political leanings as early as 1919 while still a teenager, playing the piano for dances at Brooklyn's Finnish Socialist Hall and fraternizing with other musicians with radical sympathies.[200] Years later he found encouragement in friends such as Strand and Bowles, as well as Clurman, who wrote to him on May 24, 1932, "It is clear to me that people like us are the real revolutionaries in America today and that we are revolutionary in our function as artists and leaders."[201]

Copland contributed a review to the Communist journal *New Masses* when the Workers Music League, an organization founded in 1931 and affiliated with the American Communist Party, published the *Workers Song Book No. 1* in 1934. Copland declared it to be "the first adequate collection of revolutionary songs for American workers." He proclaimed, "Those of us who wish to see music play its part in the workers' struggle for a new world order owe a vote of thanks to the Composers' Collective for making an auspicious start in the right direction."[202] While the Workers Music League was similar in its philosophy to the Artists' Congress, a large left-wing political organization that lobbied for artists' rights, jobs, and economic security and fought artistic and

Dorothy Norman, Harold Clurman. *Photograph, gelatin silver print, 3 1/2 x 2 1/2" (8.2 x 6.3 cm), 1942. Collection of Center for Creative Photography, University of Arizona, Tucson.*
© *Estate of Dorothy Norman.*

65

political repression, the Composers' Collective, founded in 1932 by the likes of Henry Cowell and Charles Seeger, was a small group of composers who aimed to create proletarian music—in other words, a new music for the masses. An interest in reaching wide audiences also inspired visual artists as diverse as the Social Realists and the Regionalists. Both groups would reject as elitist Paris modernism, and particularly abstraction, as they sought to create a new American art to speak to the masses.

Grant Wood (1892–1942), Young Corn. Oil on Masonite panel, 24 x 29 ⅞" (61 x 75.9 cm), 1931.
© Cedar Rapids, Iowa, Community School District, Memorial to Linnie Schloeman, Woodrow Wilson School.

Thomas Hart Benton, Grant Wood, and other Regionalists painted pictures representing ordinary agrarian life, a mythic America detached from the harsh realities of the Great Depression. Wood's *Young Corn* of 1931, even though painted during the Depression, glorified America's fecundity and the simple strength of its farmers. This painting coincides with a growing national interest in American history, folklore, and folk art, which Wood, too, embraced. It is particularly apparent in *The Midnight Ride of Paul Revere* of 1931, where

Grant Wood, Spring in Town. *Oil on Masonite panel, 26 x 24 ¹/₂" (66 x 62.2 cm), 1941. Sheldon Swope Art Museum, Inc., Terre Haute, Ind.*

Wood painted houses that look like children's toys and used a hobby horse as his model for Revere's horse.[203] The house in *Young Corn* is quite similar, and the trees recall those of a toy railroad. In *Spring in Town* (1941), Wood makes folk art part of his subject by depicting patchwork quilts drying in the sun on a clothesline. A man is planting the vegetable garden, recalling the family's rural past. Perhaps the popular perception of American folk sources in both Wood and Copland is one of the reasons many people associate Wood's pictures and

Copland's music. In this period, both sought to make their work reach a wider public and pondered how to create a distinctly American art.

It was a mass audience that Copland intended to reach when he entered a contest, announced in *New Masses* in early 1934, to set to music a poem by Alfred Hayes. The poem was entitled "Into the Streets May First," and was meant for use as a mass song at the Second Annual American Workers Music Olympiad on April 29 of that year; the song was to be performed by eight hundred voices from New York revolutionary workers' choruses.[204] Copland's submission was chosen as the winner. When he wrote to his Mexican friend Carlos Chávez a little over a year later, he remarked: "I noticed that you are beginning to play music from Soviet Russia. I should like very much to make a trip there. (Have you ever seen my Communist song 'Into the Streets May First'? It has been republished in Russia.)"[205] During the era of the Cold War and the House Un-American Activities Committee in the 1950s, Copland insisted that he had never joined the Communist Party.[206] Years later he denounced his song as "the silliest thing I did," explaining that he wanted "to prove to myself that I could write a better mass song than the next fellow."[207]

Copland's political sympathies were widely shared by many creative artists during the Great Depression of the 1930s, extending well beyond his immediate circle. They concerned themselves with the suffering of the masses and the actions necessary to produce a better society. Social Realist painters such as Raphael Soyer often captured the suffering of the downtrodden in their canvases. Soyer's view of unemployed New Yorkers in his work *In the City Park*, painted about 1934, depicts the plight of the dispossessed.

Copland's support of his friend Diego Rivera at this time suggests that, unlike some others in the Composers' Collective and

Raphael Soyer (1899–1987), In the City Park. *Oil on canvas, 38 x 40" (96.5 x 101.6 cm), c. 1934. Private collection. Reproduced with permission of The Estate of Raphael Soyer, Courtesy of Forum Gallery, New York.*

the Group Theatre, he was not a fan of Stalin. In November 1927, Rivera had allied himself with the anti-Stalinist Trotsky and the "October" group of artists who defended Trotsky's dissident point of view. Rivera was in Moscow to celebrate the tenth anniversary of the October Revolution, and while he was lecturing there, Stalin expelled Trotsky from the party on January 17, 1928; the Latin American secretariat of the Comintern ordered Rivera back to Mexico that April.[208] Rivera's watercolors of political demonstrations in Moscow, now known as the "May Day Sketches," depict the same revolutionary theme Copland treated several years later in his workers' song. In the watercolors, occasionally the workers' red banners echo the red babushkas worn by the women in the crowds.

Copland showed solidarity with Rivera when the painter's mural for Rockefeller Center provoked controversy in 1933. Depicting "human intelligence in control of the forces of nature," Rivera added a recognizable portrait of Lenin, which had not been in the preliminary cartoon for the fresco.[209]

Diego Rivera, May Day, Moscow. Watercolor on paper (from a sketchbook),
each 4 x 6 ¼" (10.3 x 16 cm), 1928. Museum of Modern Art, New York, Gift of Abby Aldrich Rockefeller.

When he refused to remove it, the Rockefellers ordered that the mural be destroyed. In a lengthy article on the dispute, Walter Pach, an artist and critic who had unsuccessfully tried to intervene with Nelson Rockefeller on Rivera's behalf, insisted, "I am confident that Rockefeller Center can survive such incitements to Communism and other dangers as are contained in Rivera's fresco if that work is shown to the public."[210] Supporting Rivera, Copland joined Pach, Ben Shahn (one of Rivera's assistants), and other friends of the muralist in giving Rivera a going-away party at the New Workers' School (at 51 West Fourteenth Street) on the evening of December 5, 1933.[211] Copland also contributed to the cost of tickets for Rivera and his wife, Frida Kahlo, to return to Mexico.[212]

Ben Shahn, a Jewish immigrant from Lithuania and just two years Copland's junior, had much in common with the composer. Both men were friends of Hart Crane; they had similar political sympathies; both had visited Paris in the twenties. Shahn appreciated music, which he depicted in both his paintings and his photographs. More than once, he chose to portray musical themes with allegorical intentions: In *Portrait of Myself When Young* of 1943, he depicted himself listening to a group of street musicians. Musical references abound in Shahn's pictures; *Four Piece Orchestra* (1944), *The Violin Player* (1947), *Silent Music* (1948), and *Nocturne* (1949) are just a few examples. Erik Johns, a companion of Copland's in the late 1940s and early 1950s, recalls that Copland especially liked Shahn's work.[213] Both Shahn and Copland admired the work of Walker Evans, who had been Shahn's friend since the late twenties, when the two shared a studio. Evans's photographs eventually inspired Copland's opera *The Tender Land* (1952–1954).

Diego Rivera, Man at the Crossroads *(Radio City mural, destroyed), 1933.*

One cause uniting Shahn and Copland was concern about social justice and abuses in the American court system. Shahn showed *The Passion of Sacco and Vanzetti*, a series of twenty-three gouaches, in April 1932 at Edith Halpert's Downtown Gallery. The trial of Nicola Sacco and Bartolomeo Vanzetti, convicted in 1921 of the murder of a paymaster and his guard in South Braintree, Massachusetts, and executed in 1927, had captured Shahn's attention after he witnessed European demonstrations against the trial's outcome. In *Bartolomeo Vanzetti and Nicola Sacco* (1931), Shahn depicted the two handcuffed together and chained, looking glum and resigned. At the same time that Shahn was expressing his concern, Copland's friend the composer Marc Blitzstein began an opera on the theme and Ruth Crawford Seeger set a poem about Sacco and Vanzetti to music for the First Annual Workers Music Olympiad in 1933.[214]

71

Carl Van Vechten, Diego Rivera and Frida Kahlo. *Photograph, gelatin silver print, 6 ¹/₂ x 4 ¹/₂" (16.5 x 11.4 cm), 1932. Detroit Institute of Arts, Founders Society Purchase, Diego Rivera Exhibition Fund. © Carl Van Vechten Trust.*

Shahn's next New York show, also in 1933, featured a second series based on another example of the miscarriage of justice, *The Mooney Case*—fifteen gouaches telling the story of the trial and conviction for bombing of California Labor leader Thomas J. Mooney. (Mooney was pardoned in 1939.)

Copland then satirized American justice in the music he wrote for *Hear Ye! Hear Ye!*, a ballet of 1934 commissioned by Ruth Page, ballet director of the Chicago Grand Opera Company, whose lawyer husband wrote the scenario. Page indicated to Copland that he was "*the* American composer."[215] Copland, clearly sympathetic with the causes Shahn had championed, commented that his music "incorporated segments of 'The Star Spangled Banner,' distorted to convey the corruption of legal systems and courts of law."[216]

Neither Shahn nor Copland could have imagined that Shahn would eventually combine political and musical imagery in a work that would touch upon Copland's own destiny. In Shahn's *Composition with Clarinets and Tin Horn* (1951), a horizontal red band and flames imply the turmoil caused by Senator Joseph R. McCarthy and others in their witch hunts to uncover Communists during the Cold War. Although subjected to red-baiting hysteria, Copland was never formally charged, although some of his friends underwent the kind of suffering Shahn alluded to by making musical instruments resemble prison bars.[217]

72

Ben Shahn (1898–1969), Bartolomeo Vanzetti and Nicola Sacco. Gouache on paper mounted on composition board, 10 ⅞ x 14 ⅝" (27.6 x 37.2 cm), 1931 Museum of Modern Art, New York, Gift of Abby Aldrich Rockefeller.

Ben Shahn, Composition with Clarinets and Tin Horn. *Tempera on panel,*
43 x 36" (109.2 x 91.4 cm), 1951. Detroit Institute of Arts.

"Imposed Simplicity"

By the mid-1930s, Copland began to expand his musical style in ways that paralleled the social consciousness of Shahn and so many others. He turned from high modernism to what he called "imposed simplicity."[218] As early as 1927, he had expressed respect for Ravel's *Bolero*, describing it as "the kind of brilliant piece everyone loves."[219] This marks a shift from his youthful creed that popular work could not be good. From 1935 to 1939, Copland taught at the Henry Street Settlement School on New York's Lower East Side. When the Settlement's music director, Grace Spofford, commissioned a work from him that could be

Rudy Burckhardt (1914–1999), Edwin Denby in New York. Photograph, gelatin silver print, *9 1/2 x 6 5/8" (24.1 x 16.8 cm), 1937. Collection of Joe LeSueur, East Hampton, New York.*

produced by young people in the school, he chose to collaborate with Edwin Denby, a librettist, poet, and dance critic whom he had first met in Germany in 1929. The result was *The Second Hurricane* (1936), which was directed by Orson Welles. Copland used American references, including a Revolutionary War folk song, "The Capture of Burgoyne."

It was through Denby and his companion the photographer, filmmaker, and artist Rudy Burckhardt that Copland met the painter Willem de Kooning, who, with his future wife, Elaine Fried, enjoyed attending concerts of Copland's music. Denby wrote to Copland in 1943, praising his *Piano Sonata* (1941) and telling him how much Elaine and Bill had admired it.[220] Years later Elaine recalled that when Copland mentioned how he was plagued by his neighbors' complaining whenever he played music late at night, Willem suggested that he get a loft "like us" and recommended an available one at 115 West Sixty-third Street, which Copland subsequently rented.[221] In the early 1940s Max Margulis, a vocal coach, writer, and cofounder of Blue Note Records, used to take Copland and the de Koonings to jazz clubs in the city.[222] Although neither of the de Koonings ever depicted Copland, Willem produced portraits of both Margulis (c. 1944) and Burckhardt (c. 1939) and a sketch of Denby (1947); Elaine later painted one of Denby (1960).

75

Willem de Kooning (1904–1997), Max Margulis. *Pencil on paper, 12 ½ x 9 ½" (31.8 x 24.1 cm), c. 1944. Collection of Helen Margulis. © 2000 Willem de Kooning Revocable Trust/Artists Rights Society (ARS), New York.*

Stuart Davis, Dancers on Havana Street. *Watercolor on paper,*
22 ³/₄ x 15 ⁵/₈" (57.8 x 39.7 cm), 1920. Private collection.

Stuart Davis, Night Club, Havana. *Watercolor on paper, 11 x 15" (27.9 x 38.1 cm), 1920. Collection Rose Art Museum, Brandeis University, Waltham, Mass., Gift of Teresa Jackson Weill, New York.*

At the time when the de Koonings and Copland were going to hear jazz together, Willem's work was usually figurative, but it would become increasingly abstract, in contrast to Copland's desire to develop more accessible music with wider audience appeal. Still, Erik Johns recalls that he and Copland visited exhibitions at Art of This Century, Peggy Guggenheim's gallery on West Fifty-seventh Street in New York, which showed abstract expressionist work by Jackson Pollock and others.[223]

But during the 1940s Copland was drawn to popular culture—including the kind of music that could be heard in a large dance hall—more than to the avant-garde. In the spring of 1941 Copland and his companion Victor Kraft traveled to Havana, partying with Rudy Burckhardt during the trip. Cuban popular culture had earlier become the subject of several watercolors by Stuart Davis, whose *Night Club, Havana* and *Dancers on Havana Street* (both painted in 1920) show the kind of nightspot that appealed to Davis and Copland alike, both of whom had also enjoyed the jazz clubs in New York. Copland responded enthusiastically to Cuban cabaret music and, in 1942, composed *Danzón Cubano*, dedicating it to his friend Burckhardt.

Billy the Kid

IN THE LATE 1930s LINCOLN KIRSTEIN, director of Ballet Caravan, commissioned Copland as composer and Eugene Loring as choreographer to create a ballet on an American theme. In seeking this goal, Kirstein gave Loring a copy of Walter Noble Burns's popular book, *The Saga of Billy the Kid*, a story set in the nineteenth century based upon the brief life of the cowboy William Bonney. To Copland, Kirstein gave some published arrangements of cowboy folk songs, six of which were to figure in the resulting ballet in the form of quotations.

These quotations from cowboy folk songs contributed to the popular and critical success of Copland's music for *Billy the Kid* (1938). Copland later reflected, "The use of such materials ought never to be a mechanical process. They can be successfully handled only by a composer who is able to identify himself with, and reëxpress in his own terms, the underlying emotional connotation of the material."[224] Copland's use of cowboy songs in *Billy the Kid* can be compared to Edward Hopper's use of a picture-within-a-picture in his painting *Hotel Lobby* (1943). This work depicts a conventional interior, on the wall of which hangs a popular Western image, framed with ornate gold, alluding to the American peaks and valleys captured by Albert Bierstadt and others in the

78

Edward Hopper (1882–1967), Hotel Lobby. Oil on canvas, 32 1/2 x 40 3/4"
(82.6 x 103.5 cm), 1943. Indianapolis Museum of Art, William Ray Adams Memorial Collection.

ABOVE: *Salvador Dalí (1904–1989), Le Piano Surréaliste. Pastel and gouache on paper, 23 5/8 x 17" (60 x 43.2 cm), 1937. Private collection. © Foundation Gala–Salvador Dalí/VEGAP/Artists Rights Society (ARS), New York.*

LEFT: *Salvador Dalí, Gondole Surréaliste sur Bicylettes en Feu. Pastel and gouache on paper, 29 1/8 x 21 1/4" (74 x 54 cm), 1937. Private collection. © Foundation Gala–Salvador Dalí/VEGAP/Artists Rights Society (ARS), New York.*

nineteenth century. This was the once heroic, now clichéd vision of the West that Hopper himself had declined to paint, even while traveling across the country in search of new subjects. The need to venture west for inspiration never possessed Copland, who liked to tell how he composed *Billy the Kid* in an apartment on the rue de Rennes in Paris.[225] He later recalled that his mother, who had spent part of her youth in Dallas, Texas, had sung cowboy songs to him when he was a child. He probably also heard some cowboy songs during the two months he had spent working in Santa Fe in 1928.[226]

Kirstein's commission to Copland for *Billy the Kid* followed their meeting at the New York salon of Constance and Kirk Askew, in the couple's brownstone on East Sixty-seventh Street. (Kirk Askew directed the Durlacher Brothers' art gallery on Fifty-seventh Street.) Among the salon's regulars were A. Everett "Chick" Austin Jr., a Harvard-educated painter who directed the Wadsworth Atheneum, Virgil Thomson, Carl Van Vechten, E. E. Cummings, the art critic Henry McBride, the choreographer Agnes de Mille, the art dealer Pierre Matisse, and various other dealers, curators, and painters.[227] The art critic Rosamund Bernier (then a college student), who accompanied Copland to one of the Askews' famous evenings, recalled that the artists Salvador Dalí and Pavel Tchelitchew were regulars there.[228] This was around the time when Dalí was producing drawings with musical themes, such as *Le Piano Surréaliste* (1937) and *Gondole Surréaliste sur Bicyclettes en Feu* (1937).

Pavel Tchelitchew (1898–1957), Constance Askew. Oil on canvas, 39 x 39" (99.1 x 99.1 cm), 1938.
Wadsworth Atheneum, Hartford, Gift of Mrs. R. Kirk Askew.

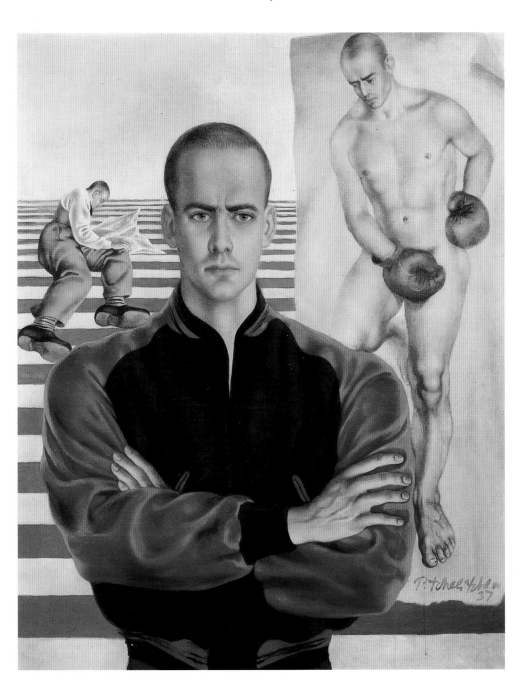

*Pavel Tchelitchew, Portrait of Lincoln Kirstein. Oil on canvas, 48 x 36"
(121.9 x 91.4 cm), 1937. School of American Ballet, New York. Photograph courtesy Jerry L. Thompson.*

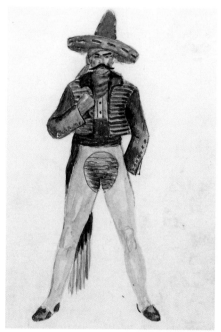

Jared French (1905–1988), Alias as Guide. Costume design for Billy the Kid. *Watercolor and pencil on paper over cardboard, 9 1/2 x 5 1/2" (24.1 x 13.9 cm), 1938. Museum of Modern Art, New York, Gift of Lincoln Kirstein.*

Jared French, Alias as Mexican. Costume design for Billy the Kid. *Watercolor and pencil on paper over cardboard, 9 1/8 x 5 1/2" (23 x 13.9 cm), 1938. Museum of Modern Art, New York, Gift of Lincoln Kirstein.*

The Russian-born Tchelitchew (who had immigrated only three years earlier), a magic realist, painted his dramatic portrait of Lincoln Kirstein in 1937 and, the next year, his portrait of Constance Askew, a haunting canvas of the hostess pondering her fleeting youth reflected both in a hand mirror and on the tabletop below, the latter recalling a death mask. Virgil Thomson recalled that "her facial carriage was . . . of a novel kind. In a time when eyes still were tightly squinted and smiles were grins, Constance Askew's relaxed visage, as calm as that of Garbo, was deeply exciting to the young men of her generation."[229]

Tchelitchew appears to have been interested in the passage of time. He depicted Kirstein simultaneously in three different modes. In the foreground, Kirstein stands boldly with his arms folded, dressed in an all-American athletic team jacket. In the middle ground he appears in an unfurled, full-length drawing as a slender nude, wearing only massive boxing gloves, one of which masks his genitals in a gesture that recalls classical sculptures of the goddess of love (such as the Aphrodite of Cnidos by Praxiteles). We see Kirstein again in the background, sprawled on the floor, dressed in a white shirt and the vest and

Jared French, Alias as Sheriff. Costume design for Billy the Kid. *Watercolor and pencil on paper over cardboard, 8 ½ x 5 ½" (21.6 x 13.9 cm), 1938. Museum of Modern Art, New York, Gift of Lincoln Kirstein.*

George Platt Lynes, Ruth Ann Koesun in a scene from Billy the Kid. *Photograph, gelatin silver print mounted on cardboard, 9 15/16 x 7 15/16" (25.2 x 20.2 cm), 1938. Dance Division, The New York Public Library for the Performing Arts, Astor, Lenox, and Tilden Foundations.*

trousers of a gray business suit, wearing glasses and reading a newspaper. Perhaps Tchelitchew hoped to convey Kirstein's virility, sexual vitality, and intellect through the threefold image.

Despite the Russian émigré Tchelitchew's obvious talent and imagination, Kirstein chose another magic realist painter, the American Jared French, whom he had only recently met, to create the decor and costumes for *Billy the Kid*. The set featured an empty prairie with cactus columns. To convey the victims of Billy's violence, Eugene Loring, the choreographer, came up with the device of having one dancer (Todd Bolender) play Alias, a character who would represent each victim, turning up again and again just after he had been shot or stabbed. French created green costumes for this chameleon figure acting out the various Alias incarnations: Alias as Mexican wore tights and (as noted on the drawings' cardboard mounts) a "satin-vest with green velvet ribbon stripes"; Alias as Sheriff No. 2 wore a felt hat and "striped shirt," while Alias as Guide wore "dark green rooster feathers," tights, and a "jersey shirt." If Kirstein did not think the Russian Tchelitchew could handle the cowboy theme, he had no doubt of the Brooklyn-born composer's ability, despite Copland's limited familiarity with the subject.

Urban Themes

A THEME CLOSER TO COPLAND'S own experience came his way the following year when, at Harold Clurman's request, he composed incidental music for Irwin Shaw's experimental play *Quiet City*. Concerning the night thoughts of various city dwellers, the play was performed only twice, by the Group Theatre in New York in April 1939, but the music survives, adapted by Copland the next year with a new arrangement for English horn, trumpet, and strings.

Wharton Esherick (1887–1970), of a great city. Wood engraving on paper, sheet size 17 ⅞ x 12 ¾" (45.4 x 32.4 cm), 1927. Whitney Museum of American Art, New York, Purchase, with funds from The Lauder Foundation, Leonard and Evelyn Lauder Fund, 96.68.97. Photograph © Geoffrey Clements, New York.

Copland's fascination with New York as the prototypical modern city parallels the work of numerous contemporary visual artists who expressed a similar enthusiasm. The designer Wharton Esherick's wood engraving *Of a Great City*, dated 1927, links the city with the creative talent it nurtures. Around the figure seated at a desk, we see books, art, and a piano keyboard, symbolizing the art generated by the stimuli of the city, its skyscrapers visible through the window. A few years later Berenice Abbott, who shared Copland's political sympathies, photographed New York in a large series that included *Night View*, shot from the

85

Berenice Abbott (1898–1991), Night View. Photograph, gelatin silver print, 13 ⅞ x 11" (35.2 x 27.9 cm), 1931–1932. Toledo Museum of Art, Ohio, Harold Boeschenstein Jr. Fund. © Berenice Abbott Commerce Graphics Ltd., Inc.

Empire State Building. But Copland was closest to Edwin Denby's companion Rudy Burckhardt, whose photograph *Flatiron in Summer* of 1947 calls to mind his first film, a short piece titled *145 West 21* (1937), in which both Denby and Copland acted; a still photograph shows the lyricist John Latouche with Copland dressed in a cap and overalls, playing the role of a roofer. The film's score was by their mutual friend Paul Bowles. A benefit screening was held at Burckhardt and Denby's loft as a fund-raiser for Copland and Denby's opera *The Second Hurricane*. Besides the film's participants, among those present were Carl Van Vechten, Lincoln Kirstein, and the artists Joseph Cornell and Alexander Calder.[230]

Rudy Burckhardt, Flatiron in Summer. *Photograph, gelatin silver print,*
11 1/8 x 9 1/8" (26.7 x 22.2 cm), 1947. Courtesy Tibor de Nagy Gallery, New York.

Urban New York again became Copland's focus when he wrote his first film score, composed to fit the five sections of a rough cut of the documentary *The City*.[231] The film premiered in May 1939, produced by Pare Lorentz, with direction and cinematography by Ralph Steiner and Willard Van Dyke, who were both known for their still photography. Shown daily at the 1939 New York World's Fair, *The City* featured Morris Carnovsky (of the Group Theatre, shown in Steiner's dramatic 1936 photograph *After the Rehearsal* with director Lee Strasberg in a maze of empty chairs and shadows) as its narrator, with

Rudy Burckhardt, Aaron Copland and John Latouche. *Film still from 145 W. 21, dir. Rudy Burckhardt, 1937. Copland Collection, Library of Congress, Washington, D.C.*

87

Film still from The City, *dir. Ralph Steiner and Willard Van Dyke (1906–1986), 1939. Museum of Modern Art, New York, Film Stills Archive.*

RIGHT: *Ralph Steiner (1899–1986), After the Rehearsal (Morris Carnovsky and Lee Strasberg). Photograph, gelatin silver print, 9 1/2 x 7 1/2" (24.1 x 19.2 cm), 1936; portfolio published 1978. Collection of Center for Creative Photography, University of Arizona, Tucson.* © *Ralph Steiner Estate.*

BELOW: *Ralph Steiner, Philadelphia Savings Bank (William Lescaze, architect). Photograph, gelatin silver print, 7 3/4 x 9 3/4" (19.7 x 24.8 cm), 1932. Museum of Modern Art, New York, gift of the photographer.* © *Ralph Steiner Estate.*

commentary by Lewis Mumford. It promoted the value of planned urban communities with green spaces. Steiner, as Denby reported to Copland, was dismayed that Mumford had insisted on cutting both the film and the score: "I suppose you know—it was cut from 3 reels to 2 without consulting Steiner or you, and Steiner is of course frantic about it (and says they've ruined the music). It is a shocking thing to do. Especially from an art-apostle like Mumford."[232] Copland, who wanted to compose film scores both to reach larger audiences and to reap the economic benefits, had seized this opportunity, a result of his long friendship with Steiner, whom he first met in 1927, the year the photographer married Mary Hughes. Denby noted that with *The City* Copland had succeeded in "cinching a Hollywood connection."[233]

Mary Hughes divorced Steiner and married the Swiss-born architect William Lescaze in 1933 but maintained a close friendship with Copland, who was thus encouraged to consider architectural modernism. Lescaze had just designed the Philadelphia Savings Bank (1932), which Steiner photographed. Lescaze not only promoted International Style architecture in America, but also painted and, like Copland, had been a friend of Hart Crane. In October 1941 Lescaze wrote to Copland to say he was glad that the composer had read and liked his new book, *On Being an Architect*,[234] in which Copland is mentioned: "Meditate on the fact that the phenomenon of one type of architecture springing up in all parts of the world is unheard of in any other art. Dreiser doesn't write like Proust; Marin doesn't paint like Rivera; Copland doesn't compose like Stravinsky."[235] Along with Copland, Steiner, Strand, Dorothy Norman, and many others sympathetic to left-ist ideals, Lescaze avidly supported the Group Theatre. He eventually advised Copland on the design of a studio in Ossining, New York, and designed a house for Norman, where Gerald Sykes, Copland and Clurman's close friend from the 1920s, was to meet his future wife, the painter Buffie Johnson.[236] (Copland recalled running into the couple in May 1955 in Paris and having Clurman come over from London for a reunion.)[237]

89

Buffie Johnson (b. 1912), Gerald Sykes. Oil on Masonite, 20 x 16" (50.8 x 40.6 cm), 1950. Collection of the artist, New York.

Political Backlash

LESCAZE'S HIGH MODERNISM was not then the primary esthetic Copland pursued. He sought greater accessibility in his own work of this period through populist subject matter. Commissioned by folk music collector Alan Lomax to write an orchestral arrangement of an American folk song for a CBS radio program aimed at a high school audience, Copland selected John and Alan Lomax's transcription of "John Henry," the ballad of an African-American steel driver who worked laying railroad tracks in the late nineteenth century. Copland's orchestration (1940) included the sound of a train and John Henry's hammer, scored for triangle, anvil, sandpaper blocks, train whistle, and piano, as well as a chamber orchestra. Thomas Hart Benton, steeped in folk music from his travels around the country, had commented on "the various 'John Henry' songs" in his book *An Artist in America*, published in 1937.[238]

A few years later, the legendary figure of John Henry also caught the attention of Palmer Hayden, an African-American artist who painted a series of twelve canvases telling the story of the hero's adventures. In *John Henry on the Right, Steam Drill on the Left* (1947), Hayden depicted Henry pitting his strong arms against the speed of a steam pile driver; Henry wins the contest but perishes in the effort. Despite the fact that this heroic character of a working man from the American frontier became associated with the Popular Front (the Soviet Union's attempt in the mid-1930s to promote antifascist culture), Copland revised "John Henry" in 1952 so that it could be played by high school orchestras.[239]

Whatever appeal the Popular Front had held for them earlier in the 1930s, Copland and his friends were dismayed by Stalin's announcement, in August 1939, of a Soviet nonaggression pact with Nazi Germany. But like many Americans on the left who became disillusioned with the Soviet government, Copland held on to his idealism, as did the Social Realist painter Joseph Hirsch, a decade younger than Copland, who maintained a commitment to humanitarian values, preferring to make art that was always accessible while others around him turned toward abstract painting. His canvas *Editorial* (1942) suggests his empathy for ordinary workers, two of whom are shown taking a break for lunch, a smoke, and a chance to ponder news of the war. Because Hirsch and Copland shared this vision of society, it is not surprising that the two got along when they met at the MacDowell Colony in September 1956, just three years after Copland had been interrogated by Senator McCarthy about his political activities. As a result of their acquaintance at MacDowell, Hirsch produced a sensitive charcoal portrait sketch of Copland, which he inscribed, "Small hommage [sic] to a large composer from Joseph Hirsch."

ABOVE: *Joseph Hirsch (1910–1981), Editorial. Oil on canvas, 18 x 26" (45.7 x 66 cm), 1942. University of Arizona Museum of Art, Gift of C. Leonard Pfeiffer.*

LEFT: *Joseph Hirsch,* Aaron Copland, September 1956. *Charcoal on paper, mat opening 13 x 10 7/16" (33 x 26.5 cm), 1956. Copland Collection, Library of Congress, Washington, D.C.*

Anti-Communist paranoia motivated Congressman Fred E. Busbey of Illinois to question Copland's political associations and prevent his *Lincoln Portrait* of 1942 from being played as part of Dwight Eisenhower's inaugural concert in January 1953, only months after the House Un-American Activities Committee hearings and the year of the McCarthy committee's Senate interrogations.[240] Copland's playwright and screenwriter friend Clifford Odets from the Group Theatre made a painting he titled *Senator Crapsey*, a caricature of a self-inflated politician advertising his own "patriotism" while persecuting others. But Odets, who, unlike Copland, had been a Communist Party member during most of 1935, agreed to name names when testifying before the House Committee in the spring of 1952.[241]

For years Odets and Copland explored collaborating on an opera, with Odets commissioning, in 1939, *Piano Sonata* (1941), which Copland dedicated to him. Then, sometime in 1951, Odets offered to commission another work from Copland, in exchange for which he offered the composer "a fine Klee."[242] (Harold Clurman recalled Odets's large collection of paintings, including several by the acclaimed Swiss modernist;[243] Aaron Siskind photographed Odets with some of his art collection, including several works by Klee, in 1950.) Copland responded to Odets's offer in October 1951, claiming that he liked the idea but did not yet know what he could do, because he was preoccupied with preparing the Norton lectures he was to give at Harvard in the spring.[244] Odets wrote to Copland again and again in the early 1950s asking if they were ever going to get together on what he referred to as "the commission–Klee picture

deal."[245] It is possible that Copland let this offer pass because he preferred more accessible art than Klee's abstract painting. By way of reference, in commenting on the frustrating aspects of the avant-garde music of Karlheinz Stockhausen that he heard in Europe in 1955, Copland speculated, "Perhaps one can say modern painting of the Paul Klee variety has invaded new German music."[246] On the other hand, Copland's lack of response to Odets's proposal may have been because it simply was not an opportune moment to accept another commission from the playwright.

Clifford Odets (1906–1963), Senator Crapsey. Watercolor, gouache, and ink on newsprint, 7 3/4 x 7"" (19.7 x 17.8 cm), c. 1950. Estate of Clifford Odets, Courtesy Michael Rosenfeld Gallery, New York.

Wartime Works

THE ABSURDITY OF THE POLITICAL harassment aimed at Copland is clear, for his *Lincoln Portrait*, a thirteen-minute work for narrator and full orchestra, was the result of a commission by the conductor André Kostelanetz just days after the bombing of Pearl Harbor in December 1941, and was clearly patriotic. Copland, guided by Kostelanetz's urging that he choose a statesman as his theme, selected Abraham Lincoln. Speaking years later to the composer Phillip Ramey, Copland insisted that he viewed this piece as "a portrait of Lincoln, pure and simple, meant for a large audience and special occasions."[247]

Copland's choice of Lincoln has its parallels in literature, the theater, and the visual arts. Since the 1920s Lincoln, identified with homespun simplicity,

93

Daniel Chester French (1850–1931), Seated Lincoln. Bronze, 32 3/8" x 27 1/2" x 28 1/4" (82.2 x 69.9 x 71.8 cm), 1924–1925. August Heckscher Collection, Heckscher Museum of Art, Huntington, N.Y., 1959.350.

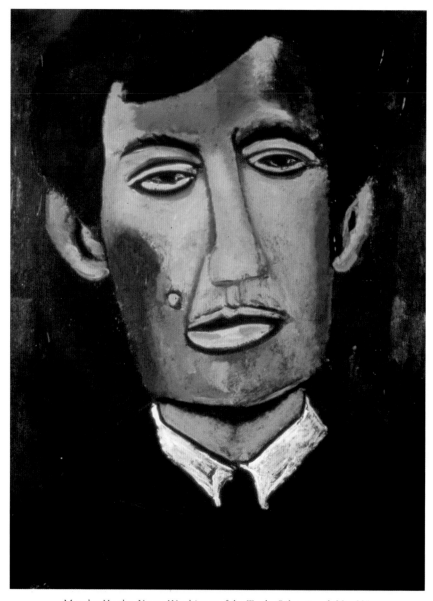

Marsden Hartley, Young Worshipper of the Truth. *Oil on panel, 28 x 22"*
(71.1 x 55.9 cm), 1940. Sheldon Memorial Art Gallery and Sculpture Garden, University of Nebraska,
Lincoln, Nebraska Art Association Collection, Nelle Cochrane Woods Memorial, 1976.N-348.

had been seen as personifying American democracy. There was the enduring popular image of the *Seated Lincoln*, sculpted in 1924–1925 by Daniel Chester French for the Lincoln Memorial in the nation's capital. Somewhat later there was Robert E. Sherwood's play *Abe Lincoln in Illinois*, a hit on Broadway in 1938, and, in 1939, the publication of the concluding volumes of Carl Sandburg's

95

Marsden Hartley, Weary of the Truth. *Oil on academy board, 28 ½ x 22 ½" (72.4 x 57.2 cm), 1940.*
Yale University Art Gallery, New Haven, Gift of Donald Gallup.

biography of the sixteenth U.S. president, which further emphasized Lincoln's heroic role during the Civil War.[248] Marsden Hartley had painted several important portraits of Lincoln, including *Young Worshipper of the Truth* and *Weary of the Truth*, both of 1940. And both Hartley and Copland certainly would have been familiar with Walt Whitman's stirring elegy to Lincoln, inspiration of

Roger Wood, scene from Rodeo *(with Jenny Workman, Dorothy Scott, Paula Lloyd, and Ruth Ann Koesun). Photograph, gelatin silver print, 8 x 7 ¼" (20.7 x 18.7 cm), 1942. Dance Division, The New York Public Library for the Performing Arts, Astor, Lenox, and Tilden Foundations.*

the sort that led Copland to compose music that fit the emotional needs of wartime America. The result was an enormous popular response to *Lincoln Portrait*, with Carl Sandburg's reading one of the most memorable.

Wartime provided the impetus for the choreographer Agnes de Mille's collaboration with Copland, for she sought to create for the transatlantic Ballet Russe de Monte Carlo "an American ballet on an American theme by an American."[249] The result, *Rodeo* (1942), was a popular success for both de Mille and Copland. Themes of cowboys and the American West appeared in the cinema and in works by visual artists both before and after Copland undertook

Roger Wood, scene from Rodeo. *Photograph, gelatin silver print, 7 ⁷⁄₈ x 10" (20 x 25.4 cm), 1942. Dance Division, The New York Public Library for the Performing Arts, Astor, Lenox, and Tilden Foundations.*

this "cowboy" ballet. One example is Mary Anita Bonner's print *The Circular Cowboy* of 1929. Copland drew upon cowboy songs he found in the Lomaxes' anthology *Our Singing Country*, such as "Sis Joe" and "If He'd Be a Buckaroo by His Trade."[250] The tremendous splash *Rodeo* made led to de Mille's work on the Rodgers and Hammerstein musical *Oklahoma!* Copland, with *Rodeo*, had once again succeeded in making his music accessible to a broad public.

The war effort also prompted Copland's *Fanfare for the Common Man* (1943), one of eighteen fanfares for brass and percussion commissioned by Eugene Goossens and the Cincinnati Symphony. Again, Copland composed music that would capture the popular imagination, even beyond his own expectations. His choice to dedicate his fanfare to "the common man" may have been inspired by the exhibition *American Folk Art: The Art of the Common Man in America, 1750–1900*, which had taken place at the Museum of Modern Art in 1932. In his emphasis on American folk art and in his catalogue essay, the curator of the show, Holger Cahill, provided a model for Copland, like those contemporary American visual artists who were discovering in the creative products of their nation's folk culture "esthetic value of a high order . . . which gave them a certain kinship with modern art."[251]

During World War II a number of artists on the political left turned to American folklore, as had the Regionalists before them. Promoting folk heroes and national myths of patriotism seemed like a means to counter fascist ideology and promote democracy.[252] For Copland, folk music offered "an authentic expression of American experience" that Cahill admired in folk art.[253] Copland later commented, "In all the arts the Depression had aroused a wave of sympathy for and identification with the plight of the common man."[254] In Copland's desire to achieve "an affirmative tone," he later used *Fanfare for the Common Man* "in an expanded and reshaped form in the final movement" of his *Third Symphony* (1944–1946).[255]

Mary Anita Bonner (1887–1935), The Circular Cowboy. Etching and aquatint on toned paper, 16 1/2 x 16 1/2" (41.9 x 41.9 cm), 1929. Witte Museum, San Antonio.

Appalachian Spring

FOR ANOTHER WARTIME PROJECT, Copland drew upon the folk music of the Shakers, a utopian religious sect that, at its height in 1840, boasted six thousand members spread over eighteen communities in the United States. He adapted a motif from their hymn "Simple Gifts" for the ballet score he composed at the request of the choreographer Martha Graham.

During the course of their collaboration, Graham sent Copland several scripts. By May 16, 1943, she was calling the project "House of Victory." She described the ballet as "a legend of living in the AMERICAN PLACE," which calls to mind both the theme and the name of Stieglitz's last gallery. She outlined a scene inside and outside a house with a doorway, a front porch, and a rope swing. On the porch was to be "a Shaker rocking chair with a bone-like simplicity of line."[256] Graham noted that the character of the Mother, whom she then intended to sit in the rocking chair throughout the piece, was "theatric in the way American Primitives are." In imagining the overture for the ballet, Graham evoked American folk paintings once again when she compared the Mother to "an American Primitive, small and perfectly drawn in costume and position."[257] Having emphasized her interest in folk culture, she then told Copland that he need not use folk material "except as you see fit."

Although Graham played down her wish that Copland incorporate American folk material in his ballet score, her various scripts for what became *Appalachian Spring* (1944) are filled with such references. She has the character of the Mother say, "Spring comes early this year, daughter. About time for spring planting, son."[258] This evokes several of Grant Wood's paintings with which Graham must have been familiar; surely she had seen his *Spring in Town* (p. 67) reproduced on the cover of the April 18, 1942, issue of *The Saturday Evening Post*. She remarked in one version of her script on "the spare beauty of fine Shaker furniture," noting, too, that "Grant Wood has caught it in some of his things."[259] His *Young Corn* (p. 66), *Spring Turning* (1936), and *Spring in Town* all address this theme. The latter work, according to Wood, "was inspired by a new appreciation of an America tranquil in a warring world, of democracy free and hopeful, of a country worth preserving."[260] Wood had earlier emphasized American folklore for patriotic reasons in his painting of George Washington cutting down the cherry tree, *Parson Weems' Fable* of 1939, about which he commented, "In our present unsettled times, when democracy is threatened on all sides, the preservation of our folklore is more important than is generally realized."[261] Wood then cited an article by the scholar and professor Howard Mumford Jones entitled "Patriotism—But How?," which argued that America needed to promote patriotism through its national

Arnold Eagle (1909–1992), scene from first performance of Appalachian Spring *(with Martha Graham, Erick Hawkins, and company). Photograph, 1944. Courtesy Isamu Noguchi Foundation, Inc., New York.*

mythology.[262] Both Wood and Graham sought patriotic images of renewal in a war-torn world.

Like the story in Graham's script, Wood depicted a small town, where connections to American tradition and rural life remain unbroken. A man plants his garden, while a woman is seen hanging out on a clothesline her patchwork quilts, a folk art form practiced even today in rural Appalachia.[263] Graham focused attention on this region where such craft traditions and folk songs have survived by taking her title from a line in Hart Crane's poem *The Bridge*. She chose the words "O Appalachian Spring!" from a section of the poem called, appropriately enough, "The Dance," in a narrative entitled "Powhatan's Daughter," about a young Indian girl, "Pocahuntus."[264] Graham's initial versions of the script included the figure of an Indian girl, who she told Copland had been inspired by both Crane's poetry and William Carlos Williams's book *In the American Grain*.[265] The title of the ballet in Copland's mind as he worked was simply "Ballet for Martha."[266] Not until the dress rehearsal did he learn what

Side table, 1800–1825.
Anonymous photograph, n.d.
Sheeler Collection, Hancock
Shaker Village, Pittsfield,
Mass., 65-244.

101

Charles Sheeler (1883–1965), interior of Sheeler's Ridgefield, Conn.,
home. Photograph, gelatin silver print, 9 5/8 x 7 1/2" (24.4 x 19.1 cm),
1939. Museum of Modern Art, New York, SC 85.238.

Charles Sheeler, Meeting
House Window, Mt. Lebanon
Shaker Village. Photograph,
6 x 8 1/4" (15.2 x 21 cm),
c. 1934. Lane Collection,
Museum of Fine Arts, Boston.

Graham had chosen to call it, although she admitted that Crane's poem actually had nothing to do with the piece. Still, her choice did not displease him, because of his long admiration for Crane's work.[267]

Graham's taste for folk culture coincided with Copland's own longstanding interest. Thus encouraged, he found in a recently published collection of Shaker tunes the hymn he would make famous.[268] Just two years earlier, Constance Rourke's book *The Roots of American Culture* had appeared, a collection of essays in which she extensively discussed the Shakers. She observed that "Music played a conspicuous role in Shaker life from the beginning . . . "[269]

Not surprisingly, a number of Copland's American contemporaries, most notably the painter and photographer Charles Sheeler, shared his fascination with the Shakers. (Sheeler was the subject of a 1938 biography by Rourke and may have stimulated her interest in Shaker culture.)[270] Like Copland, Sheeler

102

Charles Sheeler, Interior. *Oil on canvas, 33 x 22" (83.8 x 55.9 cm), 1926. Whitney Museum of American Art, New York, Gift of Gertrude Vanderbilt Whitney, 31.344.*

was attracted to the simplicity of the Shaker esthetic; he collected nineteenth-century Shaker furniture, such as the side table now at Hancock Shaker Village, and sometimes depicted aspects of Shaker design in paintings such as his *Interior* (1926), and in photographs such as that of his Ridgefield, Connecticut, home (1939) and *Meeting House Window, Mt. Lebanon Shaker Village* (c. 1934). Founded in New Lebanon, New York, in 1787, this communal settlement was the spiritual center of the sect. The Shaker esthetic appealed to the modernist sensibility because it eliminated the superfluous and made simplicity the key, creating an almost abstract design. Like Copland's music and the Shaker hymn he drew upon, Graham's modern dance esthetic was outside the nineteenth-century Romantic ethos of European tradition.

Copland said of Graham, "she's unquestionably very American."[271] He later told the composer Phillip Ramey that "*Appalachian Spring* would never

103

Isamu Noguchi (1904–1988), rocking chair for set of Appalachian Spring. *Bronze copy (cast 1965) of original wood, height 40 1/2" (102.9 cm), 1944. New School University, New York. Photograph by Shigeo Anzai, courtesy Isamu Noguchi Foundation, Inc., New York.*

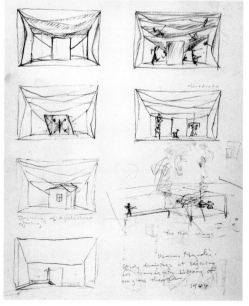
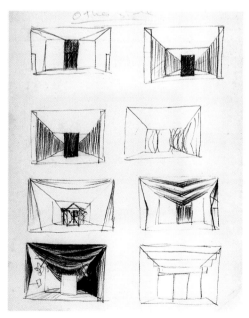

Isamu Noguchi, sketches (recto and verso) for dance set for Appalachian Spring. *Pencil on paper, 11 1/8 x 9 3/8" (28.3 x 23.8 cm), 1944. Isamu Noguchi Foundation, Inc., New York.*

have existed without her special personality. The music was definitely created for her, and it reflects, I hope, the unique quality of a human being, an American landscape, and a way of feeling."[272] Visual artists, too, responded to Graham's personality, including Paul Meltsner, who painted a dramatic image of her in a dance pose, and Isamu Noguchi, who sculpted her portrait. It was Noguchi whom Graham commissioned to create the sets for the ballet; about her he commented, "*Appalachian Spring* was in a sense influenced by Shaker furniture, but it is also the culmination of Martha's interest in American themes and in the puritan American tradition."[273]

Graham had been investigating "the American" in dance since the early thirties, influenced by her teacher, Ted Shawn, who expressed his interest in Native American and African-American influences.[274] Shawn wrote, "If the dance in America is going to reach the heights that it should, we must as a nation produce composers to keep pace with what we are doing in the world of dance."[275] Yet when Agnes de Mille invited Shawn to hear Copland and the young Leonard Bernstein play the newly finished score of her forthcoming ballet *Rodeo* at Jacob's Pillow in 1942, he refused to attend, renouncing their music.[276]

Paul Meltsner (1905–1966), Martha Graham. Oil on canvasboard, 20 x 16"
(50.8 x 40.6 cm), 1938. Courtesy Michael Rosenfeld Gallery, New York.

Composing for Film

BACK IN 1919, YEARS BEFORE EITHER Graham or de Mille had dreamed up "American" ballets, Waldo Frank had summed up his view of American mass culture: "The true popular Theater of the American masses is, thus, the Movie. Before the Movie, the American masses had no theater. The whole world now has its cinemas. America alone has nothing else. America alone has nothing better."[277] Thus Copland, like many other important composers, wanted to write film scores, about which he noted, "Composing music for film is not in itself 'easier' than writing concert music except that the form, length, and general tone are set in advance, so the composer does not have to make those initial decisions."[278]

Copland's first commission to compose music for Hollywood came for Lewis Milestone's *Of Mice and Men* (1939), based on the 1937 novella by John Steinbeck. In Copland's eyes, the film offered "an American theme, by a great American writer, demanding appropriate music."[279] When he returned to New York after six weeks in Hollywood working on the score, he lectured about

105

Film still from Of Mice and Men, *dir. Lewis Milestone, 1939. Museum of Modern Art, New York, Film Stills Archive.*

composing for the cinema at the Museum of Modern Art and wrote articles about his Hollywood experience.[280] He reflected on the value of music in a film, on its ability to link visual and narrative aspects: "Music, an art which exists in time, can subtly hold disparate scenes together. In exciting montage sequences where film moves violently from shot to shot, music by developing one particular theme, or one type of rhythmical material, or some other unifying musical element, supplies the necessary continuous understructure."[281]

ABOVE: *Film still from* The North Star, *dir. Lewis Milestone, 1943. Museum of Modern Art, New York, Film Stills Archive.*

RIGHT: *Film still from* The Red Pony, *dir. Lewis Milestone, 1949. Museum of Modern Art, New York, Film Stills Archive.*

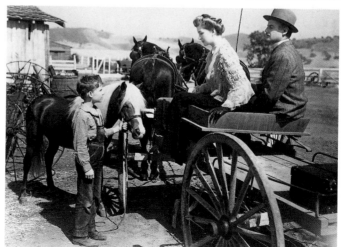

Copland's score for *Of Mice and Men* received two Academy Award nominations, for best score and best original score. His experience composing for Milestone was so positive that the two collaborated on two more films: *The North Star* (1943, after Lillian Hellman's play) and *The Red Pony* (1949, after John Steinbeck's story). *The North Star*, a film about Ukrainian peasants before and after the Nazi invasions, was released in October 1943, "just before Russia became an enemy instead of an ally," according to Copland.[282]

107

ABOVE: *Film still from* The Cummington Story, *dir. Helen Grayson and Larry Madison (for U.S. Office of War Information), 1945. Museum of Modern Art, New York, Film Stills Archive.*

LEFT: *Film still from* Our Town, *dir. Sam Wood, 1940. Museum of Modern Art, New York, Film Stills Archive.*

Copland also composed film scores for *Our Town* (1940, after Thornton Wilder's play), the Office of War Information's documentary *The Cummington Story* (1945), William Wyler's *The Heiress* (1949, after Henry James's *Washington Square*), and Jack Garfein's *Something Wild* (1961, after Alex Karmel's *Mary Ann*). The score of *The Heiress* won Copland an Academy Award. The continuing appeal to film directors of his work is exemplified by Spike Lee's use of Copland's music for his movie about basketball, *He Got Game* (1998). Lee commented that he got the idea while writing the script, noting, "When I listen to his music, I hear America, and basketball is America."[283]

RIGHT: *Film still from* The Heiress, *dir. William Wyler, 1949. Museum of Modern Art, New York, Film Stills Archive.*

BELOW: *Film still from* Something Wild, *dir. Jack Garfein, 1961. Museum of Modern Art, New York, Film Stills Archive.*

Actor Denzel Washington on cover of CD brochure for motion picture soundtrack to He Got Game, *dir. Spike Lee, 1998. Sony Classical SK60593.*

Postwar Years and Beyond

COPLAND'S OWN IMAGE OF AMERICA shifted over the years. He explained that he saw Emily Dickinson's work as related to folk culture: "Her poetry, written in isolation, was folklike, with irregular meters and stanzas and many unconventional devices."[284] According to Copland, his decision in 1949 to compose music for twelve of her poems began with "The Chariot," which opens:

> Because I could not stop for Death,
> he kindly stopped for me;
> the carriage held but just ourselves
> and immortality.[285]

The initial public reception to these songs was not as successful as he had hoped; Copland's biographer Howard Pollack has called them "part of a trend away from public statements toward more private ones," attributing this shift to postwar disillusionment and to developments in Copland's personal life, including his move out of Manhattan.[286]

109

In the early 1950s, during the time he had to counter the aggressive investigations of Senator McCarthy, Copland focused on composing *The Tender Land*, an opera on the subject of rural poverty in America during the 1930s, inspired by James Agee and Walker Evans's collaborative book of 1941, *Let Us Now Praise Famous Men*.[287] Two of Evans's photographs, those of Allie Mae Burroughs and her ten-year-old daughter, Lucille, served as inspiration for Erik Johns, Copland's companion of this period, who wrote the libretto under the pseudonym Horace Everett.

When they met in 1946, Johns was a modern dancer who also painted. He sometimes sketched and photographed Copland, catching his distinctive profile and calm demeanor. At Tanglewood in the summer of 1952, Johns depicted Copland at the piano with Irving Fine, the young composer to whom Copland had dedicated one of his Dickinson songs, looking on. Johns's sketch of Laurie Moss, the tenant farmer's daughter in *The Tender Land*, appears on the cover of the published opera.[288] Standing before a picket fence and looking out across the landscape, anticipating graduation, the girl "dreams of a larger life" (p. 112).

Gradually, Copland began to compose less and to spend more time conducting, first his own music, then, in 1951, another composer's work, David Diamond's *Rounds*. Copland admitted, "I always felt that composing was the really serious business; conducting was for fun. But it has other advantages: It keeps one young, and it pays the bills."[289] He had encouraged the young Leonard Bernstein to train professionally as a conductor.[290]

Walker Evans (1903–1975), Alabama Cotton Tenant Farmer's Wife (Allie Mae Burroughs). Photograph, gelatin silver print, 8 ⅛ x 6" (20.5 x 15.3 cm), 1936. FSA (Farm Security Administration) Collection, Library of Congress, Washington, D.C.

Walker Evans, Lucille Burroughs, Daughter of a Cotton Sharecropper, Hale County, Alabama. *Photograph, gelatin silver print, 8 1/8 x 6" (20.5 x 15.3 cm), 1936.* FSA Collection, Library of Congress, Washington, D.C.

111

Copland met Bernstein's friend the artist Larry Rivers, recalls Erik Johns, who accompanied him to a party at Rivers's studio on Fourteenth Street. It was the younger composer Lukas Foss (who had arranged *Billy the Kid* for solo piano) and his wife, the painter Cornelia Foss, who had first introduced Bernstein to Rivers. The result was a lasting friendship and several portraits of Bernstein, including one on music notation paper (p. 113). But Rivers never came to know Copland well.

Another prominent figure in the visual arts, Alexander Calder, commissioned Copland to compose *Inaugural Fanfare* for the dedication in 1969 of his sculpture *La Grande Vitesse* in Grand Rapids, Michigan (p. 114). The large-scale public sculpture, known as a stabile (as opposed to Calder's kinetic mobiles), was the first ever to be jointly commissioned and financed by federal and private funds.[291] Erik Johns remembers that Copland particularly "responded to sculpture."[292] Copland explained that he "knew and admired Sandy Calder and this was a spectacular sculpture, so I accepted the commission."[293] Calder described the square heads of his specially designed bolts, which hold his giant red metal sculpture together, as reflecting "a simple form that relates to the common man,"

Erik Johns (b. 1927), Aaron Copland and Irving Fine at Tanglewood. *Pencil on paper, 12 x 8" (30.5 x 20.3 cm), 1952. Collection of Jack Gottlieb.*

Erik Johns, *cover illustration for* The Tender Land, 1956. *Collection of Erik Johns.*

perhaps alluding to Copland's *Fanfare for the Common Man.*[294]

Both Copland and Calder had previously collaborated with Martha Graham and had achieved parallel status as significant figures in American culture. In fact, the program for the dedication of *La Grande Vitesse* reprinted an article from *Art in America,* "Calder's International Monuments" by Robert Osborn, who wrote of the sculptor, "Calder is all American. Apple pie type."[295] Such a declaration appears carefully constructed to counter any argument that a modernist abstract esthetic is not American, and the fact that Calder was then spending much of his time at his home in Saché, France. Not surprisingly, the program for the dedication emphasized the American aspect of the event by including, in addition to Copland's fanfare, Charles Ives's *Variations on "America"* and Robert Russell Bennett's arrangement of a "symphonic synthesis" of George Gershwin's *Porgy and Bess.*

Following the fanfare for Calder, in 1973, on commission for the Van Cliburn Competition, Copland composed a melancholy piece, *Night Thoughts (Homage to Ives).* He had long admired Ives, whose songs of 1919–1921 he judged "a unique and memorable contribution to the art of song writing in America."[296] Although Copland had essentially ceased

Cornelia Foss, Portrait of Lukas Foss. Pencil on paper, 10 x 8" (25.4 x 20.3 cm), c. 1980. Collection of the artist. Photograph courtesy Jim Strong.

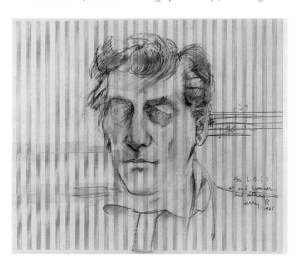

Larry Rivers (b. 1925), Portrait of Leonard Bernstein. Pencil on music notation paper, 13 ¾ x 15 ¾" (34.9 x 40 cm), 1965. Private collection.

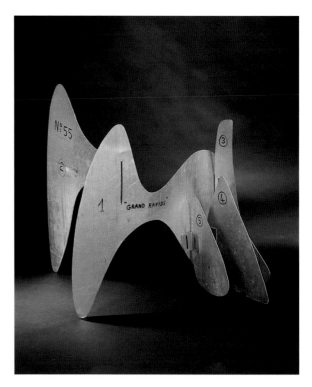

114

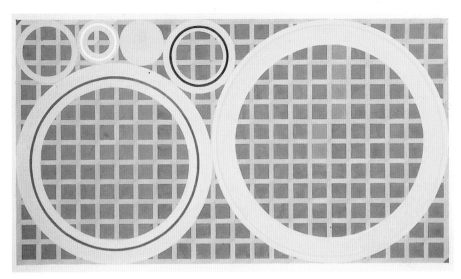

Richard Hennessy (b. 1941), Gardens of China. *Casein on paper, 12 ⅞ x 23" (33 x 58.2 cm), 1967. Copland Heritage Association, Cortlandt, N.Y.*

115

composing by the late 1970s, his friend Phillip Ramey (whom he first met in 1967), together with the pianist Bennett Lerner, encouraged him to publish three short piano pieces based on earlier sketches: *Midsummer Nocturne* (1947, 1977), *Midday Thoughts* (1944, 1982), and *Proclamation* (1973, 1982).[297]

Even in old age, Copland maintained friendships with several distinguished visual artists. The sculptor Louise Nevelson and the painter Elaine de Kooning were among the guests present on August 16, 1984, at the party for the publication of the first volume of his autobiography.[298] Nevelson, who was born in Russia, responded to a recording Copland sent her of his *Vitebsk*, commenting that she listened to it "with relish."[299]

In addition, over the years Copland developed intimate friendships with a number of younger visual artists, including Alvin Ross and Richard Schiff.[300] Copland saved a pencil sketch Schiff made of him on music notation paper (dated October 1957) and the artist's rather expressionistic ink and pencil sketch of the

John Chamberlain (b. 1927), Untitled. *Painted metal, 8 ¾ x 9 ½ x 8 ½" (22.2 x 24 x 21.6 cm), c. 1965. Collection of Richard Hennessy.*

composer at the piano in his study in 1958.[301] Copland also befriended and even collected the work of the painter and critic Richard Hennessy, among others.[302] Several of Hennessy's artworks remain in the collection at the Copland Heritage Association in Cortlandt, New York.

Collecting art was suggested to Copland by Erik Johns, who recalls that in the 1960s, Copland had a painting by Ben Nicholson on approval from a New York gallery, but thought it too much responsibility and returned it. Richard Hennessy took Copland to the Leo Castelli Gallery and encouraged his purchase of a small sculpture by John Chamberlain, which he kept on a table in his living room. In 1980 the painter Paul Jenkins gave Copland a monograph on his work, which he inscribed, "For Aaron Copland Whose sounds have allowed us to hear that which was not there before."[303] The two men had exchanged visits after appearing on the same television program, one produced by the United States Information Agency.

Edvard Lieber, who works in both music and the visual arts, recalls visiting Copland in 1984, just after the publication of a recording of his music. Lieber's recording was brought to Copland's attention by their mutual friend (and Copland's long-time supporter) Minna Lederman Daniel, who had published Copland's articles and Alfred Frueh's caricature of him (p. 120) in *Modern Music*. Lieber remembers that Copland told Minna that he found Lieber's *Prelude to Jackson Pollock's "Autumn Rhythm"* "a miracle of compression" and that he would like to meet Lieber, who subsequently drove up to spend the day with Copland and played his "Pollock" piece for him on the piano.[304]

Rhoda Sherbell (b. 1938), Phillip Ramey.
Bronze, 8 1/2 x 9 1/2 x 4 1/2" (21.6 x 24.1 x 11.4 cm),
1976. Collection of the artist.

117

Richard J. Schiff (1932–1968), Aaron Copland at the Piano. Ink and pencil on cardboard, 8 x 12" (20.3 x 30.5 cm), 1958. Copland Collection, Library of Congress, Washington, D.C.

Conclusion

AS I BEGAN TO LOOK FOR LINKS between Aaron Copland and the visual arts, I thought of seeking clues among the images chosen for the jackets of his recordings. But before I could press this early intuition, it was overshadowed by the abundance of material my research turned up in other directions. Only as I was finishing this text was I able to make the pilgrimage to a secondhand shop in the Midwest that I knew harbored a rich collection of magazines and records. Three albums that I found in the bins in the dim basement offer a welcome counterpoint to discoveries I made more conventionally in libraries and archives.

Since I had confirmed through the Library of Congress evidence that Martha Graham had called Copland's attention to Grant Wood in her unpublished script for *Appalachian Spring*, I was delighted to see that a designer had intuitively chosen a painting of Wood's, *Stone City*, for the cover of a 1975 Columbia Masterworks recording of Copland's music conducted by the composer himself.[305]

Having investigated the impact of Leo Ornstein and cubism on the young Copland and included a cubist portrait of Ornstein by William Zorach in this exhibition (p. 13), I was pleased to discover that this same painting had been chosen for the cover of a 1981 album, *Cadenzas and Variations*, featuring music by Copland, Ornstein, Philip Glass, and Richard Wernick.[306]

The third album offered an even more complex parallel to my discoveries and the theme of this exhibition. This album, a 1959 recording on the Everest label of Copland conducting the London Symphony Orchestra in his *Third Symphony*, features a cover by the noted graphic designer Alex Steinweiss. A photograph of a landscape fills the background, with hills, fields, a road, and barn that could have been painted by Grant Wood. In the foreground, cut off from the landscape by a low wooden deck wall, stands a rough table. On it to the right are a white pitcher of flowers, tubes of paint, brushes, and an artist's palette smeared with paint. To the left stands an easel, on which the painter has represented neither the rural landscape beyond the deck nor the conventional still life close at hand. The pitcher does appear in the artist's composition, but distorted, angular, in cubist style, and the rest of the canvas sports a scrap of newspaper, a playing card, a detached balustrade floating in space, and so on: In short, it is a classic cubist collage. The designer evidently sensed that modernist experiments and contrasting esthetics in the visual arts offered parallels to Copland's musical interests and developments. We have seen how he moved between modernism and folk cultures, jazz, and the cinema in his search for an American national art.

The album notes quote Copland's comment that his *Third Symphony* (composed from 1943 to 1946) "contains no folk or popular material. During the late twenties it was customary to pigeon-hole me as a composer of symphonic jazz, with emphasis on the jazz. More recently, I have been catalogued as a folklorist and purveyor of Americana. Any reference to jazz or folk material in this work is purely unconscious." Responding to this statement, Paul Affelder, author of the album notes, called attention to the symphony's "unconscious references, not necessarily to jazz or folk material but most certainly to that characteristically American quality of Copland's melodic line which predominates his ballet and film scores."[307] It is this perception of an "American quality," shared by so many, that has become our subject, one that continues to intrigue.

PICTURING AARON COPLAND

Gail Levin

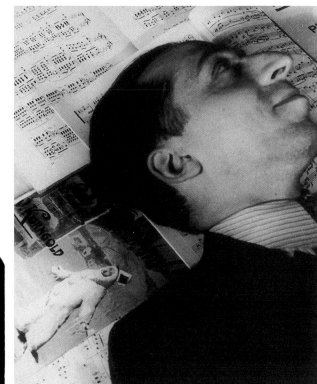

120

Alfred Frueh (1880–1968), Aaron Copland.
Caricature published in Modern Music, 1924.
Copland Collection, Library of Congress,
Washington, D.C.

Carl Van Vechten, Aaron Copland. Photograph,
gelatin silver print, 1932. Copland Collection,
Library of Congress, Washington, D.C.
© Carl Van Vechten Trust.

WITH ITS DISTINCTIVE PROFILE, Aaron Copland's face attracted eminent
artists and photographers throughout his career. Among the earliest was Alfred
Frueh, who produced a linear caricature of the young Copland in 1924 for the
journal *Modern Music*. Its editor, Minna Lederman Daniel, described to Vivian
Perlis how "striking" Copland was in appearance:

> For artists and photographers he was always the perfect subject, the
> face one could never forget—after Stravinsky's, THE face. All in
> all he had, as the cartoonist Al Frueh said, a triangular look. A long,
> lean body gave the perfect balance to his impressive beaked head.
> Even then there was an air of unstudied elegance about him.
> A hawk, yet not predatory.[1]

George Platt Lynes, Aaron Copland. *Photograph, gelatin silver print, 12 ⁵/₁₆ x 10 ¹/₄" (31.3 x 26 cm), 1935. Beinecke Rare Book and Manuscript Library, Yale University, New Haven.*

Naomi Savage, Portrait of Aaron Copland at Tanglewood. *Photograph, gelatin silver print, 9 ¹/₂ x 7 ¹/₂" (24.1 x 19.1 cm), 1949. Collection of the artist, Princeton, N.J.*

In the early 1930s Carl Van Vechten made a number of photographs of Copland, sometimes posing him rather formally against meaningful backgrounds like an American patchwork quilt (p. 50) or, as here (p. 120), sheets of music. To create this image, Van Vechten assumed a dramatic vantage point from above his subject, capturing him in stark profile. A much less dramatic but no less striking photograph of Copland is Ralph Steiner's 1933 portrait (p. 148) showing the composer in casual dress, seated in a relaxed pose in front of a rough wooden barn door—a background that, like the quilt in Van Vechten's earlier photo, suggests a "homespun," distinctly American quality. Capturing Copland's face in three-quarter view, Steiner emphasized his friend's beaked nose and his intensity.

George Platt Lynes took a deliberately theatrical approach to some of the portraits he made of Copland in 1935, posing him in his New York studio set

Erik Johns, Aaron Copland at Snedens Landing.
Photograph, 10 x 8" (25.4 x 20.3 cm), 1951.
Collection of Erik Johns.

Erik Johns, Aaron Copland. Ink marker on paper,
7 x 5 ½" (17.8 x 14 cm), 1951. Collection of
Erik Johns.

seated in a canvas director's chair that he had used for many other subjects. Lynes's various shots include a view of Copland face forward, his arms folded in his lap (p. 8); a profile view from the same session but with especially dramatic lighting shows Copland with his left hand raised pensively to his chin (p. 121). In this image, the multiple shadows his figure casts on the wall behind him suggest the complex personality of a creative individual.

Radically different from this approach was the one Naomi Savage adopted when she photographed her distinguished subject at Tanglewood in the summer of 1949 (p. 121). Omitting all context, she portrayed Copland in a close-up profile view against a light ground, cropping his head at the top. He appears to glance downward, underlining the meditative mood Savage caught. Just two years later, in 1951, Erik Johns, Copland's companion at the time, depicted the

Aline Fruhauf (1907–1978), Aaron Copland.
Pencil and blue ink on paper, 9 ³/₁₆ x 6 ³/₈"
(23.3 x 16.2 cm), 1962. National Portrait Gallery,
Smithsonian Institution, Washington, D.C.

Aline Fruhauf, Aaron Copland. Woodcut on
paper, 10 ¹/₁₆ x 3 ¹/₈" (25.6 x 7.9 cm), 1962.
Copland Collection, Library of Congress,
Washington, D.C.

composer's profile in a drawing and a photograph that seem to show him in a casual air, comfortable with himself.

While in residence at the MacDowell Colony in the fall of 1956, three years after he had been interrogated about his political activities by Senator McCarthy, Copland met the Social Realist painter Joseph Hirsch. The two men shared political sympathies; both were committed to humanitarian values and to creating art accessible to all. Hirsch's charcoal portrait of Copland from this period (p. 91) is a careful and sensitive study, reflecting a camaraderie quickly forged by like-minded artists. He seems to have caught the playful aspect of Copland's personality noted by so many of his friends.

Gordon Parks set out to depict Copland in 1958 with the idea in mind of conveying that sense of place so many have associated with his music. Thus, he

Marcos Blahove (b. 1928), Aaron Copland. Oil on canvas, 27 7/8 x 31 7/8" (70.8 x 81 cm), 1972. National Portrait Gallery, Smithsonian Institution, Washington, D.C.

chose to photograph his subject posed in front of a characteristically American barn (p. 2). Although it is unlikely that Parks knew Ralph Steiner's earlier portrait of Copland in front of a barn door, both photographers sought to project the same association of the composer with Americana. Yet because Parks photographed him formally—dressed in a suit and tie, wearing his glasses, and resting his hands on an open notebook with a pen at the ready—he caught a number of contradictions in Copland's public image. The composer pictured here is at once both the sophisticated urban modernist and the people's folksy champion of Americana.

In a 1959 portrait of Copland (p. 119) Arnold Newman followed his usual environmental style, photographing his subject in the context of his work. Just as

Mervin Honig (1920–1991), Rhoda Sherbell Sculpting Aaron Copland. Color photograph, 1977. Collection of Rhoda Sherbell.

Rhoda Sherbell, clay model for cast metal sculpture, Aaron Copland—Dean of American Music. Bronze, 20 $^{11}/_{16}$ x 10 $^{1}/_4$ x 10 $^{5}/_8$" (52.6 x 26 x 27 cm), 1977. Heckscher Museum of Art, Huntington, N.Y., 1999.25.

he often posed visual artists with their paintings or sculptures, he depicted Copland in profile in front of sheets of music on a stand. Newman's decision to show Copland's head in sharp focus against a soft background gives the composer's unmistakable profile a sculptural feel, emphasized by the palpable texture of his hair, wrinkled skin, and tweed jacket. It is unlikely that Newman knew of Van Vechten's earlier photograph of Copland in profile against a sheet of music; in any case, Newman's straightforward perspective contrasts with Van Vechten's tricky camera angle.

If Arnold Newman caught physical reality, Aline Fruhauf projected personality in her lively 1962 caricature of Copland conducting (p. 123, original drawing and woodcut made from it). Her image of Copland is closest to that

Irving Penn (b. 1917), Aaron Copland. Photograph, gelatin silver print, 10 ⁹/₁₆ x 10 ⁹/₁₆" (26.9 x 26.8 cm), 1979. National Portrait Gallery, Smithsonian Institution, Washington, D.C., gift of Irving Penn. © CBS, Inc.

earlier caricature by Frueh, and also recalls another by Al Hirschfeld, whose drawings of the composer have graced the covers of at least two recordings of his music. Copland's features were a caricaturist's dream.

Marcos Blahove's 1972 portrait of Copland (p. 124) is the only oil painting for which the subject is known to have posed. Blahove depicted Copland in three-quarter view, seated in an armchair, with his hands clasped and raised to his chin. In this image, the composer seems tranquil and engaging.

In 1977 Copland sat for sculptor Rhoda Sherbell in his studio in Peekskill, New York, so that she could complete work on a life-size clay model of his head that subsequently would be cast in bronze. The occasion was documented by Mervin Honig's photograph of the artist with her subject (p. 125). Recalling Copland's "infectious giggle," Sherbell remembered a moment when his dog, a

Edvard Lieber (b. 1948), Aaron Copland. *Photograph, 1984. Collection of the artist.*

Great Dane named Nadia Boulanger, entered the studio and went directly to the sculpture, affectionately kissing the piece and licking off the clay that formed the right nostril, provoking Copland to grab her and insist, "I'm over here."[2]

Hans Namuth's 1979 portrait (p. 128) shows Copland dressed casually in a turtleneck, arms folded. He looks at the photographer provocatively and seems to suppress a grin, giving us a glimpse of his impish nature. Another 1979 portrait, by Irving Penn, depicts the composer again in a turtleneck, this time in profile, with glasses resting on his forehead, eyes in shadow, and hand supporting his chin. Edvard Lieber's 1984 photo shows him in profile but looking in the other direction.

This fascinating sequence of images lets us see Copland becoming himself. It is fortunate that so many excellent artists made him their subject, giving us a changing view of the man who in turn gave us the lasting legacy of his music.

THE MUSIC OF
AARON COPLAND

Judith Tick

THE MUSIC *can have an extraordinary grandeur, an exquisite delicacy, a prophetic severity, a ferocious rage, a sharp bite, a prickly snap, a mystical suspension, a wounding stab, an agonized howl—none of which corresponds with the Aaron we loving friends know; it comes from some deep, mysterious place he never reveals to us except in his music.*[1]

Leonard Bernstein, 1979

THE CURRENT STATE of Aaron Copland's musical legacy is so fraught with contradiction that it evokes an old admonition: Be careful about what you wish for, because you may get it. Throughout his long, illustrious career, Copland rejected the stereotype of the artist as a "high priest of art," consistently reaffirming the social purpose and cultural relevance of the American composer of classical music.[2] He wished for a body of music that expressed a distinctively American consciousness. Today, he is represented in society at large by a few powerful musical icons that have been exported into mass culture through the media. "Simple Gifts," the Shaker tune immortalized in his ballet *Appalachian Spring*, opens a television newscast. "Hoe-Down," from another ballet, *Rodeo*, is used as the score of promotional commercials for the beef lobby. *Fanfare for the Common Man* heralds the ceremonies of corporate-sponsored competitive sports. So, in a sense Copland got part of what he wanted, for he is now widely acknowledged for creating an "American sound" in classical concert music. Here the ironies begin.

LEFT: *Hans Namuth (1915–1990), Aaron Copland. Photograph, 1979. Copland Collection, Library of Congress, Washington, D.C. © Hans Namuth Ltd.*

Much of Copland's oeuvre—a body of about 100 works—remains relatively unknown outside the specialized world of modern American classical music. To be sure, some of it has entered the repertory of performers, and virtually all of his output can be found on compact disks. Still, live performances of the majority of Copland's solo and chamber music occur more sporadically than routinely. Until fairly recently, English rather than American critics paid the most attention to his work. In the classical music academy, Copland's fame has helped perpetuate the ease with which his legacy has been diminished and misunderstood. Contemporary values are sometimes imposed negatively on Copland's vaunted Americanist mission, and his cultural nationalism is rendered suspect for allegedly promoting chauvinism or imposing a homogeneous identity on a diverse society—as if the Depression and home-front cultures of the 1930s and 1940s should be judged by today's affluent cultural pluralism. Furthermore, it is a sad commonplace of the Copland literature to divide his style into the categories of "serious" and "popular," the former ranking higher than the latter. Although Copland himself supplied the vocabulary for such a division by writing about his "imposed simplicity" as "the way out of isolation for the contemporary composer," he grew increasingly uncomfortable with what he recognized as overstatements about his alleged split personality as a composer.[3] ". . . [F]or the sake of drawing sharp distinctions you rather overdo the dichotomy between my 'severe' and 'simple' styles," he told a composer friend. "The inference is that only the severe style is really serious. I don't believe that."[4] He knew that what made his music so "American" also sustained his radical mind.

As an artist who considered André Gide his favorite writer, Copland embraced Gide's idea of "la part de Dieu," the "unconscious part" of a work that plays so powerful a role in "exteriorizing" (Copland's word) through art the imagination and desire within. Surely, Copland's affinity for Gide was reinforced by their mutual homosexuality and Gide's public acknowledgment of his own sexual nature during a time of pervasive homophobia. But more pertinently, Copland respected the unknowable and mysterious threads of attachment between an artist's inner self and his outer modes of expression, and he relied on Gide to help guard the gates of his creative privacy. Once, when asked to explain the "spirit" of a particular work, Copland responded, "What that particular spirit is, is not for me to say. In another connection, André Gide has well expressed my meaning: 'Before explaining my book to others, I wait for them to explain it to me. To wish to explain it first would be to restrain its meaning prematurely, because even if we know what we wish to say we cannot know if we have said *only* that. And what interests me especially is what I have put into my book without my own knowledge.'"[5] In other words, Copland tolerated and, indeed, expected multiple interpretations of his work.

Years of Exploration

IN 1939, FACING THE MILESTONE of a fortieth birthday, Copland began a memoir by constructing an autobiographical landscape of his birth. *When* he was born is never directly stated. Instead, he lavishes detail after detail on the *where*:

> I was born on a street in Brooklyn that can only be described as drab. It had none of the garish color of the ghetto, none of the charm of an old New England thoroughfare, or even the rawness of a pioneer street. It was simply drab. It probably resembled most one of the outer districts of lower middle-class London, except that it was peopled largely by Italians, Irish, and Negroes. I mention it because it was there that I spent the first twenty years of my life. Also, because it fills me with mild wonder that a musician was born on that street. Music was the last thing anyone would have connected with it. In fact, no one had ever connected music with my family or with my street.[6]

131

Place continued to serve as a metaphor for discovery in more autobiographical reflection some ten years later. In a set of public lectures delivered in 1952, he said:

> The instinctual drive toward the world of sound must have been very strong in my case, since it triumphed over a commercially minded environment that, so far as I could tell, had never given a thought to art or to art expression as a way of life. . . . My discovery of music was rather like coming upon an unsuspected city—like discovering Paris or Rome if you had never before heard of their existence. The excitement of discovery was enhanced because I came upon only a few streets at a time . . . Music was like the inside of a great building that shut out the street noises. They were the noises natural to a street; but it was good to have the quiet of the great building available, not as a haven or a hiding place, but as a different and more meaningful place.[7]

If Copland went on to create some of the most memorable soundscapes of American experience, it was because of his own awareness of the relationship between creativity and environment, his own need for the imaginative mind as a refuge. His memories of boyhood Brooklyn bear witness to his sensitivity to place as a touchstone for the self.

Yet looking backward at his own looking backward, from the distance of the present, one might also "wonder mildly" about the verisimilitude of his own description of the cityscape of his birth. Was Copland skewing the realities of Brooklyn to recreate the familiar myth of American achievers, who emerge from humble incongruity? His street, left unnamed, was Washington Avenue, often described by others as an attractive urban thoroughfare and a middle-class haven of respectability.[8] His family (whose very ethnic group Copland omitted from his own survey) were Eastern European Jews, who owned an upright piano that allowed Copland's sisters to take music lessons. Copland's parents, Harris and Sarah, had emigrated as young children from Russia in the mid-1870s, his father changing Kaplan to Copland along the way, and his mother living in Illinois and Texas before landing in the Bronx. The Coplands—Aaron was the youngest of five children—lived above a mid-size department store that they owned and where Aaron worked as a boy. He would remain forever aware of, and more often than not bemused by, the seeming contradictions in his own personality—indeed in his own musical compositions—calling himself "thoroughly bourgeois" and at the same time living the life of the "bohemian."

Born into the moderate success story of many Jewish immigrants, Copland would make his own story, in part, deliberate Jewish assimilation. He was surrounded by relatives—fifteen aunts and uncles either born or brought here, separated in his mind by "the way they spoke—with or without a foreign accent." Copland further candidly acknowledged how this "may have had something to do with my later stressing the need for a specifically American speech in our serious music."[9] Confronting the indifference of his parents to his own musical education, he arranged for his first piano lessons when he was eleven. By seventeen he found his first composition teacher.

From 1917 to 1921 Copland went into Manhattan for theory and composition lessons with Rubin Goldmark (1872–1936), an eminent composer and teacher. Goldmark was famous for having studied with the great Czech composer Antonín Dvořák, whose tenure at the National Conservatory in New York (1892–1894) yielded not only his *New World Symphony* but also several influential and controversial proclamations about the need for American classical composers to study indigenous folk musics, in particular Negro songs (plantation songs) and Indian melodies. (In this he perhaps unwittingly singled out the two most oppressed minorities in the country at the time.) In turn, Goldmark produced orchestral works such as *Hiawatha Overture, Negro Rhapsody,* and *The Call of the Plains,* whose titles Copland would later describe as revealing "a certain need to identify his music with the American scene."[10] Even if we know little else about how much of Dvořák's openness to vernacular music Goldmark transmitted to Copland, through students such as Goldmark (and Will

Marion Cook), Dvořák "indirectly pointed the way for a younger generation of Americanist composers, among them Duke Ellington and George Gershwin."[11]

Goldmark gave Copland a solid training in nineteenth-century German practice, which in the manner of the precocious young artist, Copland both assimilated and rejected. Not for him the veneration of the great Romantics, whom he regarded not as "universal" but as German. While he learned conventional harmony and classical forms, Copland listened avidly to music by composers with idioms oppositional to German style: the Russian composers Mussorgsky and Scriabin and the French masters Debussy and Ravel. He also heard music by the young Americans John Alden Carpenter and Charles Griffes, and long remembered the sensation caused by the pianist-composer Leo Ornstein, a rare, prewar Russian-born American rebel whose solo recitals lit brush fires under the feet of complacent critics in Europe and New York between 1914 and 1919.

Copland specifically recalled the controversy surrounding Ornstein's *Danse Sauvage*, or *Wild Men's Dance* (1913).[12] Ornstein composed this four-minute solo piano work mainly in "note-clusters," his term for the dissonant conglomerates so thickly stacked with notes as to require special notation in the published score. He occasionally played note clusters with the palm of his hand, marking them fortissimo (very very loud) and il più marcato possibile (as accented as possible). How seriously the young Copland took this "enfant terrible" (who, notwithstanding, dedicated *Wild Men's Dance* "to my dear 'MUMS'") is not entirely clear. Possible skepticism is suggested by a letter from his close friend Aaron Schaffer:

133

> Your account of the Ornstein recital was interesting because of the fact that that musician-clown seems to have produced rather much the same impression upon you as he did upon me, when I heard him some two years ago. I shall never forget the amused snicker that passed over the audience as he rose completely from his seat to pound the crashing discords of his "Anger."[13]

The label "Futurism" clung to Ornstein then and has since. (The New York music critic James Huneker once wrote that Ornstein was "the only true-blue, genuine Futurist composer alive.")[14] Musical "Futurism" meant a willingness to compose with sounds usually considered noise, outside the realm of acoustic instruments and organized pitch. More conservative than Italian Futurist machine experimenters, such as Luigi Russolo, who wrote a manifesto titled *The Art of Noises* (1913), Ornstein pioneered an approach to the grand piano as a percussive machine, capable of grinding out fierce dissonances and assaulting rhythms.[15] It is not inconceivable that some seed for the hard-as-nails articulation Copland adopted in his later *Piano Variations* (1930) might have taken root in Ornstein's music.

"Futurism" was only one of the many iconoclastic esthetics and isms in the air. The language of classical music was in transition, extricating itself slowly from the tonal and harmonic principles developed between Bach and Wagner, and a system called "tonality" or "functional harmony," which relied on the hierarchy of major and minor keys. After 1900, tonality (centering a musical composition around one key) increasingly became an option rather than a premise. Such enormous destabilization was akin to the transition between representative and abstract painting. It would have repercussions for the rest of the century.

"Those were the impressionable years of exploration," Copland later wrote.[16] His apprenticeship between 1917 and 1921 resulted in some twenty works for small chamber ensembles, solo piano, and voice that show his discoveries. Copland described much of it as influenced by French music, singling out a *Prelude* for violin and piano as "somewhat in the style of César Franck," and three songs in the style of Debussy.[17] He mined the erotic vein of "orientalism" in some early melancholy songs, among them "Spurned Love" and "Alone."[18] Two piano works from this period display the beginnings of Copland's own voice. In *Humoristic Scherzo: The Cat and the Mouse* for piano (1920), a whimsical hide-and-seek game is played through unusual eclectic harmonies: The piece opens up with a pentatonic fragment (for the cat), and scampers in the upper registers of the keyboard with Debussyesque whole-tone harmonies and volatile upper-range piano patterns that recall Ornstein's *Mood for Piano* titled "Anger." Copland's eclectic idiom delights the ear by mixing and matching glassy French arabesques, abrasive chords, and even some melting back-lit consonance.

Copland's piano piece "Jazzy," the third in a set of three *Moods for Piano* (1920–1922), lets in the sounds of commercial popular music and illustrates the composer's lifelong habit of working in quotations from vernacular music.[19] Hits from Broadway shows and ragtime were piled up in sheet music on the upright piano in the Coplands' parlor, where his sister Laurine played for the family. Copland learned the latest dance steps from his sisters, and recalled how at the home of cousins in the Bronx who had a phonograph that his house lacked, he "would sit for hours with my ear to the horn listening to popular records."[20] "Jazzy" has the kinetic bounce of Tin Pan Alley ragtime pop songs, which composers like George Gershwin and Irving Berlin were popularizing on piano rolls. Copland's biographer Howard Pollack notes how the opening theme has the rhythmic profile of the song "Makin' Whoopee" (1928), composed by Walter Donaldson a few years after Copland finished his piece.[21] In fact, the slow section of "Jazzy" quotes another, earlier Donaldson hit, the tender pop song

"My Buddy" (1922). Transforming its waltz rhythms into rag syncopations and touching up its Romantic harmonies with blues, Copland may have intended the quotation of this particular pop song as an homage to a friend left behind ("My buddy, Your buddy misses you").[22] Copland entitled the piece "Jazzy" because to him, as to most urban white Americans, the word signified the presence of ragtime rhythms in popular songs; he seems not to have known the more complex ragtime styles of Scott Joplin, for example. Still, Copland's interest in popular music and "jazz" idioms (by which he meant pop-song ragtime) predated both his European experience with more sophisticated jazz and the success of Gershwin's *Rhapsody in Blue*.[23]

All this happened behind the scenes as Copland studied with the conservative Rubin Goldmark. Before allowing him to graduate from his studio, Goldmark required Copland to complete a traditional sonata. It was dutifully composed. The kind of evolutionary theme development and modulatory drama (wherein compositions travel away from a home key and then back again) that defines sonata form embodied the Germanic esthetic most alien to Copland's musical temperament; its usage would remain rare in his oeuvre. Copland left for France in June 1921. In August, Goldmark wrote him an admonishing letter: "I hope you will make some more progress in the Sonata form. Don't get to despise this, even if you should fall into the hands of some radicals."[24] It was already too late.

Paris

COPLAND ARRIVED IN FRANCE intending to spend one year and instead stayed on for three. Many factors contributed to making this period so formative for the young composer. One was his new composition teacher, Nadia Boulanger, whom he found by serendipity while enrolled at the American Conservatory at Fontainebleau during his first summer abroad. Later in life, when Copland patted himself on the back for having had "a certain amount of courage . . . to study composition with a woman," he acknowledged his great stroke of luck because "Mademoiselle Boulanger was an extraordinary musician."[25] She herself stood at the threshold of a great career as a teacher. Boulanger coupled her encyclopedic knowledge of music literature with an immense enthusiasm for and grasp of contemporary music. While her composition students naturally took private lessons, Wednesday afternoon sessions held at her apartment were devoted to group classes in musical analysis. There Boulanger ranged brilliantly over all of music literature, resurrecting lost treasures of early music, like Monteverdi, reading through a complex Mahler symphony score at the piano, and decoding the prewar revolution wrought by

135

Igor Stravinsky, whom she idolized. She demanded that her students sight-read compositions still in manuscript by contemporary French composers, some of whom occasionally even dropped by for tea. Boulanger was a living Michelin Guide to modern music. When analysis ended, a classic French salon began, visited by one-, two-, and three-star composers. Recalling an encounter with Stravinsky at one such salon, Copland said, "You can imagine the feelings of a young composer from Brooklyn shaking hands with such a famous character."[26]

Rising in the ranks of her protégés, Copland was invited to Boulanger's dinner parties as well. No opportunity was wasted. An after-dinner performance by Copland of his *Passacaglia* for piano led to a commission from one of Boulanger's dinner guests, the New York Philharmonic conductor Walter Damrosch, who later premiered Copland's *Symphony for Organ and Orchestra* in 1925, with Boulanger at the keyboard. (Copland incorporated the tune "Au Clair de la Lune" into the scherzo movement as a bit of fun.) In the spring of 1923 Boulanger took Aaron Copland to the home of another one of her great friends, the Russian émigré conductor Serge Koussevitzky, who was about to embark for the United States on what would be his twenty-five-year tenure as conductor of the Boston Symphony Orchestra. That meeting launched a lifelong friendship between the two men. American classical composers have had few greater allies than Serge Koussevitzky, who helped sustain Copland's entire career, eventually performing twelve of Copland's orchestral works and recording many of them.[27] Boulanger's confidence in Copland also stemmed from her belief that "American music was about to take off," as Copland's friend and Paris compatriot-composer Virgil Thomson later wrote.[28] Paris made an ideal site for a runway.

Outside Boulanger's studio, Copland took advantage of the rich musical life of Paris. He experienced the most progressive music and the most progressive esthetics at the same time. He went to cabarets and clubs featuring American jazz, for the French public as well as the avant-garde had been fascinated with American popular culture since World War I. The brilliant concerts organized by Serge Koussevitzky between 1920 and 1924 also left their mark, and there Copland heard Honegger's *Pacific 231* and Stravinsky's *Octet* and *Piano Concerto*. "Only in the atmosphere of Paris in the twenties could an orchestral series like that have taken place, and with such expectation and popularity," Copland later wrote.[29] Stravinsky replaced Debussy and Scriabin as Copland's choice for the most important modern composer, and Copland repeatedly paid homage to Stravinsky's three classic ballets, *The Firebird (L'Oiseau de Feu)*, *Petroushka*, and *The Rite of Spring (Le Sacre du Printemps)*, both in his music and his writings about music. Some twenty years later, Copland would write how Stravinsky's orchestration "had no rivals for brilliance and exhilaration," and that

"*Le Sacre du Printemps* remains, after forty years, the most astonishing orchestral achievement of the twentieth century."[30]

The enormous prestige of Stravinsky's pre–World War I ballets was sustained in Paris by the Ballets Russes. Copland attended its famous world premiere of Stravinsky's *Les Noces (The Wedding)* in 1923. The Ballets Russes had a rival in the adventurous but lesser-known Swedish Ballet (Ballets Suédois), famous for producing spectacles of sound, cubist scenery, and fervent ideas. Copland's very first night in Paris had found him at the world premiere of the Swedish Ballet's performance of *Les Mariés de la Tour Eiffel (The Wedding Party at the Eiffel Tower)*, a satire of bourgeois manners. With a scenario by Jean Cocteau, *Les Mariés* inspired Cocteau's famous manifesto *Le Coq et l'Arlequin*, celebrating "une musique de tous les jours" ("everyday music") and promoting the debunking anti-Romantic models of music hall and circus as an expression of modernist attitude. The collaborative score for *Les Mariés de la Tour Eiffel* introduced Copland to five of the six composers known as *Les Six*: Georges Auric, Arthur Honegger, Darius Milhaud, Francis Poulenc, and Germaine Tailleferre. Of these, Milhaud won Copland's greatest admiration. Copland wrote many years later that he was "a pushover for anything Milhaud signs."[31] Other productions he attended included two more ballets with complete scores by Milhaud—*L'Homme et Son Désir (Man and His Desire)* and *La Création du Monde (The Creation of the World)*. Still famous for its adroit and innovative use of jazz-derivative themes and instrumental timbres, the latter work has since entered the concert repertory; Copland particularly admired its jazz-themed fugue.[32] The trendiness of jazz was reinforced that evening by the second ballet on the program of *La Création*'s premiere, *Within the Quota*, which featured an American-authored scenario (by Gerald Murphy) and a score by a young American composer, Cole Porter.

Daytimes Copland would return to Boulanger's studio and work hard at assimilating Paris's new sounds. During his study with Boulanger, he completed several composition assignments, including *Four Motets* for a cappella mixed chorus, *Passacaglia* for piano, and "As It Fell Upon a Day," a setting of a seventeenth-century poem for voice, piano, and two clarinets, which is his best-known work from this period. His most obscure work—unjustly so—is an unstaged ballet, *Grohg*. (Although Copland recycled music from *Grohg* into the *Dance Symphony*, only in the 1990s was the complete ballet score reconstructed and recorded for the first time.)[33] As the most ambitious work from Copland's Paris years, as well as his first extended score and first orchestral work, *Grohg* allows us to review his progress as a composer up to this point.

Urged by Boulanger to write a ballet, Copland began composing plotless dances during the summer and early fall of 1922, which he spent in Berlin. After

137

he and his friend Harold Clurman saw the classic German expressionist vampire film *Nosferatu*, Clurman, who would later found the Group Theatre in New York, agreed to write a scenario (script for a ballet) based on the film. And so *Grohg* was born. In a thirty-minute ballet only dimly related to *Nosferatu*, the peculiarly named Grohg is a magician who brings corpses back to life to watch them dance and obliquely fulfill his murky desires for love and companionship. Copland's ballet begins with a "cortège," a ghostly procession of coffins borne by the "servitors," or slaves, of Grohg. Then follow in succession dances for an adolescent, an opium eater who responds to "visions of jazz," and a streetwalker moving to a distorted waltz. The climax of the ballet is given over to Grohg's hallucinations and rages.

Grohg shows a virtuoso orchestrator in the making. Notable in particular is Copland's deft handling of wind and brass instruments: Grohg's theme, when played by a solo high bassoon, turns a wild thing into a lonely plaintive creature. Here is a gesture Copland would return to often in his career, repeatedly taking advantage of the silky sound of woodwinds as a group and the objective lyricism of solo oboe, flute, or bassoon to evoke a range of emotions from tranquility to alienation. A neo-classical sense of order and proportion, which Copland absorbed from Boulanger, pervades this work. In addition, we hear all the harmonic tricks of the post-tonal trade that Copland assimilated, among them "octatonic" scales built on successive whole and half steps, and "bitonality" and "polytonality," associated in particular with Stravinsky and Milhaud. Copland defined these as "the idea of sounding two or more separate tonalities simultaneously," which reaffirmed tonality rather than destroyed it.[34] Copland's American identity comes out in his jazz-based idioms. Blues-infused themes appear in the "visions of jazz" section danced by the opium eater and in the asymmetrical

Aline Fruhauf, Nadia Boulanger. *India ink, pencil, and gray wash with blue chalk and opaque white on paper, 8 1/8 x 3 3/8" (20.6 x 8.6 cm), 1960. National Portrait Gallery, Smithsonian Institution, Washington, D.C.*

waltz of the streetwalker, where Copland bends a pitch into a quarter tone in a viola solo. Innovative volcanic polyrhythms of jazz shape several exciting climaxes, particularly in the finale. This technique, which Copland regarded as one of the most important musical idioms jazz had to offer the classical composer, deserves comment. Defining polyrhythms as "two or more independent rhythms at the same time,"[35] Copland wrote that "at its best moments it [jazz] partakes of a true independence of different rhythms sounded simultaneously."[36] In the bars of Paris and Vienna, where he heard African-American musicians, Copland realized that jazz rhythms might be a malleable idiom for making music with a distinctive American sound. Boulanger even may have pushed him into such insight, for she was the first to point out that he "had a rhythmic sense that differed from that of the Europeans."[37] To be sure, Copland knew and had used jazz before he reached Europe. Nevertheless, in *Grohg* he combined the neo-primitivist effects of Stravinsky's rhythmic drive with jazz's rhythmic ingenuities.

The ironies of an American composer awakening more fully to jazz abroad rather than at home have not been lost on many commentators. Yet they miss the point. As Copland later explained:

> My years in Europe from the age of twenty to twenty-three made
> me acutely conscious of the origins of the music I loved. Most of the
> time I spent in France, where the characteristics of French culture
> are evident at every turn. The relation of French music to the life
> around me became increasingly manifest. Gradually, the idea that
> my personal expression in music ought somehow to be related to my
> own back-home environment took hold of me. The conviction grew
> inside me that the two things that seemed always to have been so
> separate in America—music and the life about me—must be made
> to touch. This desire to make the music I wanted to write come out
> of the life I had lived in America became a preoccupation of mine in
> the twenties.[38]

The alienation of his Brooklyn boyhood, where "music and the life about" me did not touch[39] echoes in the language of his search for cultural connections. Copland had the quintessential experience of the American abroad, feeling the clarifying otherness that comes from being an outsider in countries where cultural patrimony is treasured and ethnic homogeneity taken for granted. Jazz would have echo effects across his whole career; if, in subsequent years, he would learn to value it as art, at this point he considered it vernacular source material, supplying mediating idioms between international modernism and his own desire to express a distinctive American consciousness.

New York Modern

IN JUNE 1924 COPLAND CAME HOME to New York and began to shape his career. What a splash this virtual unknown made in the next two seasons! Without any prior performances of his music in the United States, Copland received two world premieres from two major American orchestras. In January 1925, Damrosch premiered the *Symphony for Organ and Orchestra* with the New York Symphony Orchestra. In 1927 Koussevitzky brought the *Piano Concerto* to Boston. So meteoric was his rise that by 1928 a Los Angeles interviewer described Copland as "internationally famous."[40] In 1929 he and four other composers split the astronomical prize money of $25,000 in a competition sponsored by the RCA Victor Company for the best American symphony, for which he recycled *Grohg* into the *Dance Symphony*. Nevertheless, Copland lived a spartan existence, surviving some years better than others on a mixture of commissions, fellowships (two Guggenheims, several stays at the MacDowell Colony), financial support from patrons and friends, and part-time teaching at the New School for Social Research. Not until his work as a Hollywood film composer in the late 1930s would he enjoy any real financial security.

As a cultural milieu, New York by the mid- and late 1920s was cosmopolitan and vibrant. Great virtuoso performers began their national tours at Carnegie Hall or made famous debuts at the Metropolitan Opera. New York "[is] undoubtedly the musical center of the world," Sergei Rachmaninoff claimed, flattering audiences he had come to conquer in 1929.[41] Amid so much activity, young American composers struggled to make opportunities for their new music to be heard. In contrast to Paris, where salons of the rich centered the modernist scene, composers in New York took the American route and organized. Within ten years they founded the International Composers' Guild, the League of Composers, chapters of the International Society for Contemporary Music in both New York and Chicago, and a Pan American Association of Composers. Along with Koussevitzky, the conductor Leopold Stokowski programmed new symphonic American works as well. Newspapers and trendy magazines like *The New Republic*, *Vanity Fair*, and *The Dial* paid fresh attention to musical modernism at home and abroad. By 1929 the influential modernist culture critic Paul Rosenfeld wrote:

> We have an American music: there existing a body of sonorous work,
> not jazz, made by persons associated with the American community,
> to be grouped without impertinence with classic European works. . . .
> As a whole, the musical movement is still slighter and of less
> importance than either the pictorial or the literary, in proportion to

its comparative recency. But it exists; it swells. New creative talents appear with every year . . . How many revelatory experiences do we not owe to the work of Varèse, of Chávez, and Copland?[42]

Copland threw himself into this "musical movement." In the mid-1920s he found a milieu and allies among New York women, in particular, who were fostering the new music movement as patrons, writers, and executive administrators. Alma Morgenthau Wertheim, who founded Cos Cob Press in 1929 in order to promote American composers, was Copland's first major American publisher.[43] Auditioning for the League of Composers in 1924, Copland soon involved himself as a board member and contributing critic for its journal, *Modern Music*, edited by Minna Lederman. In Claire Reis, the executive director of the League of Composers, Copland made his most important ally. A conduit to such figures as Paul Rosenfeld and the writer and cultural critic Waldo Frank, Reis had earlier helped Leo Ornstein's career. Now it was Copland's turn to be sustained by what Frank described as her "luminous nourishing energy."[44] Copland and Reis shared a missionary zeal to promote modernist music. As the music historian Carol Oja has written, Reis "felt the social mission of a Jane Addams or Lillian Wald" in advocating the cause of modernist music.[45]

141

Copland consolidated his growing fame in other ways as well. From 1928 to 1931, he and his friend the composer Roger Sessions produced the Copland–Sessions series of concerts. In the 1930s he helped run concerts at Yaddo, an artists' summer residential community. In 1932 he started a Young Composers' Group. Surveying the scene, advocating for change, reviewing the latest recordings, or challenging complacent critics, Copland compiled a journalistic track record of articles and books, which in turn fed his own ambitions. He struggled to make a place for himself and his peers as they confronted not only European rivals like Stravinsky and Bartók, who in the 1920s toured and conquered the United States, but also the equally overwhelming popularity of jazz and Broadway theater.

When Copland returned from Paris in 1924, promising himself to write music with an American consciousness, he came home to George Gershwin. How prepared was he for the extraordinary sensation created by *Rhapsody in Blue*, which had premiered in New York just a few months earlier, in February 1924, with Paul Whiteman's orchestra? Back in New York by November after a national tour, Whiteman packed audiences into Carnegie Hall, Aeolian Hall, the Brooklyn Academy of Music, and the Metropolitan Opera House to hear the new "experiment in modern music"—symphonic jazz.[46] As the music historian Vivian Perlis has noted, "Only black Americans puzzled over all this, including the question of how a bandleader with the incredible name of Whiteman had come to be called 'The King of Jazz.'"[47] Gershwin's success only fueled a still-ongoing debate about black culture, which then (as now) contained elements of white racism, Eurocentric snobbery, and black cultural aspiration.

Was jazz "American" or "Negro" or a combination of the "Tin Pan Alley Jew and the Negro," and therefore not really "American" at all?[48] Was it valuable in and of itself or only as yeast for the "higher forms"? Copland's friend the critic Paul Rosenfeld dismissed jazz altogether: "American music is not jazz. Jazz is not music."[49] In his book *The Seven Lively Arts* (1924), the radical white dissenter Gilbert Seldes argued for its vitality and excellence. Within the black community the response was mixed, as a desire to vindicate black music and culture sometimes devalued jazz and blues. Among the Harlem Renaissance literati, for example, some critics initially proffered only qualified approval. In an article published in Alain Locke's pathbreaking anthology *The New Negro*, the critic Joel A. Rogers talked about jazz "being sublimated," the debt owed to it by French modernists, and quoted Serge Koussevitzky: "'It [jazz] has epochal significance—it is not superficial, it is fundamental. Jazz comes from the soil, where all music has its beginning.'"[50]

In 1925, the year he took Koussevitzky to a few jazz clubs in Harlem himself, Copland was quoted in an article titled "Jazz as Folk Music." Echoing

RIGHT: *Alma Wertheim.
Anonymous photograph,
n.d. Private collection.*

OPPOSITE: *Minna Lederman.
Anonymous photograph, 1937.
Private collection.*

Dvořák, he gave a missionary text for classical composers. "If we haven't a folk-song foundation, we must invent one," he stated, adding that popular songs and jazz be treated as generative material.[51] Two years later Copland published a long article, "Jazz Structure and Influence," in which he analyzed its polyrhythmic implications and revealed his own limitations as a jazz analyst, neither mentioning any African-American musician by name nor acknowledging the profound role played by improvisation.[52] Like many white musicians of the period, Copland made little distinction between popular musical styles that exploited ragtime and blues idioms and more authentic black musics. Still, at a time when a leading white classical-music magazine put the headline "The Jazz Problem" on its cover, Copland focused on jazz as one possible solution to his quest for American musical identity.[53] Although for him jazz would forever remain the "other," as opposed to "classical," music, he embraced jazz as a vindication of American culture. Some years later, in his notes for a lecture called "Forms of Modern Music," in which he again discussed his rival Gershwin and, again, left individual black musicians unnamed, Copland wrote, "Jazz gives us a new musical dignity."[54] Copland found his own way to use it. He demonstrated   143

its potential as an interfacing idiom between popular and classical music in several works composed between 1924 and 1930: the unduly neglected *Symphony*

for Organ and Orchestra; "An Immorality," a work for women's chorus; *Music for the Theatre*, a piece for small orchestra; and the *Concerto for Piano and Orchestra*.

These works gleam with the élan and polish of a sophisticated composer. The best, and also the best known, of this group of works is *Music for the Theatre*, which was commissioned by the League of Composers for a concert conducted by Serge Koussevitzky in November 1925. An eighteen-minute "Suite in Five Parts" for a small orchestra, *Music for the Theatre* evokes a commercial theater pit band and the wit of a Broadway revue. Instead of long, songlike themes (in the manner of Milhaud), we get motives (fragments of musical ideas) manipulated with the skill of a magician who makes cards appear and disappear at will. The "Prologue" opens with a scatting trumpet that within seconds shifts to a bluesy call-and-response with a string choir, sounding simultaneously mysterious and tender. Almost as fast a spry clarinet theme appears. A vaudeville melody in overdrive intrudes from nowhere and is gone within seconds. Oboe and muted trumpet moan low at the final cadence. More quotations of and allusions to popular idioms turn up, such as the opening motive from the late-nineteenth-century Tin Pan Alley hit "The Sidewalks of New York" in "Dance," the second part of the piece, or to stripper music in the brazen fourth part, "Burlesque."[55] "It's whorehouse music!" exclaimed the composer Roy Harris.[56] Copland said the "Burlesque" was also "partly inspired" by the singer-comedian Fanny Brice (with her famous Russian-Yiddish accent), whom he might have seen, just when he was composing this movement,[57] in a live performance in Irving Berlin's *Music Box Revue, 1924–1925*,[58] which opened a six-month run in December 1924.

Music for the Theatre is a good example of Copland's "kaleidoscopic" technique: Now you hear it, now you don't. Or else you hear the idea from a different angle. Of this work Copland explained his jazz idiom in modernist visual terms, beginning with a slam at his putative rival: "Gershwin is serious up to a point. My idea was to intensify it [jazz]. Not what you get in the dance hall but to use it cubistically—to make it more exciting than ordinary jazz."[59] The difference between Gershwin and Copland is the difference between an onstage piano player with his sleeves rolled up as one of the gang and an offstage observer, appraising the music while sipping a glass of *vin rouge*.

Yet Copland's music received very mixed reviews during these years. While some critics praised his successful integration of vernacular music into larger symphonic forms, Copland later wrote how "any piece based on jazz was assured of a mild *succès de scandale*."[60] He knew that from his own experience with Boston's reaction to the *Piano Concerto* in 1927. Newspapers kept the pot boiling over what Boston *Herald* music critic Philip Hale described as Copland's "shocking lack of taste." How dare Copland bring African-American idioms into that temple of high art, Boston Symphony Hall! Another reviewer, H. T. Parker, called him "the ogre with that terrible Concerto."[61] Copland's friend the conductor and modernist Nicolas Slonimsky mischievously mailed him the reviews. Copland tried to brush them off:

> You're a darling to have sent all those delightful write-ups. After reading them I went to the mirror to see if I could recognize myself. . . . And all that really worries me is whether or not the Maestro [Koussevitzky] will ever again have sufficient courage to perform me anywhere. . . . When the Concerto is played again ("O horrid thought!") we must see if we can't get the police to raid the concert hall to give a little added interest to this "horrible" experiment. Til soon, Aaron.[62]

At the time, Copland thought he had reached the end of the road with "symphonic jazz." Shifting course after 1928, he tried his hand at yet another kind of idiom in such works as *Vitebsk*, a trio for piano, violin, and cello; the less successful *Symphonic Ode*; and the radical *Piano Variations*. In one way or another, these works reveal a certain expressionistic attitude in Copland's oeuvre, that is to say, a search for a heightened emotional intensity available through increased dissonance or exaggerated compression of material. Copland's 1927 setting of E. E. Cummings's untitled poem that begins "in spite of everything," initially titled "Song" and subsequently "Poet's Song," influenced by the atonal approach of Arnold Schoenberg, had already foreshadowed that.

145

Copland returned to his Jewish roots in *Vitebsk (Study on a Jewish Theme)*, named for the Russian-Jewish shtetl (village) memorialized in the Yiddish play *The Dybbuk*. An acclaimed production of this play opened in New York in 1924; it was followed in 1925 by a production in English translation that Copland attended, then moved to Broadway in 1926, ending its run with a national tour.[63] As the "Jewish theme," Copland used the Hasidic *nigun* (or folk song) "Mipne Mah," which serves as the play's prologue and epilogue—so important to the play that its music was included in the publication of the script in English translation in 1926.[64] In the New York production of *The Dybbuk* that Copland saw, one famous dramatic high point was the tortured wedding dance of the haunted bride and the village beggars in the second act, treated in expressionistic style. The operetta composer Joseph Rumshinsky vividly recalled this moment as one he would "never in my whole life forget . . . grotesque and increasingly malevolent, they [the beggars] whirl around her [the bride] til she swoons."[65] Copland did not forget this moment either, later describing his own interpretation of the wedding dance in the middle section of *Vitebsk* as containing a "grotesquerie."[66] If Stravinsky's *Rite of Spring* evoked pagan Russia, Copland's *Vitebsk* evoked the primitive "harshness and drama of Jewish life in White Russia."[67] More abrasive than anything Copland had written before, *Vitebsk* has an abandon and tragic spirituality that are barely contained in its ten-minute single-movement form. Its Jewish flavor comes from a combination of the declamatory wailing of harsh dissonances that open the work and recur throughout, the use of orientalizing quarter tones, and the melancholy G-minor folk tune sung by the cello. The ending of *Vitebsk* dissolves as thematic elements are ripped out of their framework and exposed to silence. Its concluding section foreshadows Copland's minimalist tendency to deconstruct his material, to employ what the composer Ned Rorem later called Copland's "craft of 'dépouillement,' of stripping bare," that is, getting to the essence without any artifice.[68] As a metaphor for emotional compression and intensity, this new technique became increasingly explicit in subsequent works, among which the *Piano Variations* (1930) stands as a landmark.

Few works in the Copland oeuvre have the symbolic import of the *Piano Variations*, representing for some musicians a high point of his esoteric modernist style. (A "composer's composition," it became the kind of piece even his detractors admitted had some merit.)[69] Copland himself cared deeply about this piece, describing it in some detail in his writings. He explained how his manipulations of the theme of four pitches, which underlay the subsequent twenty variations, gave the piece its structural logic. Sometimes he related this to his interest in Schoenberg's serial approach and other times not, although the overall work is tonally centered in ways that Schoenberg rejected.

The *Piano Variations* has the ascetic majesty of an Arctic landscape. "Strike each note sharply," the score states about the opening theme. A later variation specifies that the melody should be played by the thumbs of both hands. Shunning conventional pianistic virtuosity, Copland compresses every ounce of possible power into a single tone. Unusual single-note or two-part textures prevail to an extraordinary extent. The melodic line—such as it is—leaps about in wide, jagged skips. Clangorous single tones and even occasional chords sound as if they are being played on stalactite pipes; they are relieved occasionally by lacy patterns tinkling in the upper registers of the piano or by melting consonance, never by any softening linear counterpoint. Responding to the label "abstract," intended as praise for this work, Copland once said, "I don't like the word 'abstract' too much . . . I don't think it's [the *Piano Variations*] really abstract. I think it's full of feeling, but not, I hope, of an obvious kind."[70] To his friend the poet Lola Ridge he wrote, "To live on—to develop means, as I see it, to enter always more and more deeply into the very essence of tragic reality. . . . there is a certain essence of contemporary reality which is expressed in the Variations. . . ." Such confidences help us understand Copland's expressionistic attitude and esthetic at this time.[71]

Political Ideals and Pragmatism

WHEN THE STOCK MARKET CRASHED in 1929, so did the network of musicians, patrons, and audience that Copland knew as the New York modern music scene. In the 1920s no idea of social relevance called any modernist ambition to account. "Previously, our works had been largely self-engendered: no one asked for them; we simply wrote them out of our own need," Copland wrote later.[72] In the midst of the Depression, such high individualism seemed self-indulgent. As the historian Richard Pells has written, "the search for personal freedom and an abstract international culture was giving way to a spirit of commitment. . . . No longer must the writer [or artist] be a pariah in his native land. The Depression gave him a chance to re-establish communication, sink roots, find an outlet for his talents, join a movement larger than himself. Above all, he might gain a sense of belonging—the greatest gift the 1930s could bestow."[73]

Over and over Copland gave that sermon to his colleagues and to the public at large. A composer's music sounded for and through the people, as he explained in 1932:

147

> A true musical culture never has been and never can be solely
> based upon the importation of foreign artists and foreign music, and
> the art of music in America will always be essentially a museum art
> until we are able to develop a school of composers who can speak
> directly to the American public in musical language which expresses
> fully the deepest reactions of the American consciousness to the
> American scene.[74]

The "American scene" in the 1930s awakened social conscience as much as consciousness. Copland, like so many other artist-intellectuals in the United States, sought connections between art and social change, and he turned to left-ist politics. Declining to join the American Communist Party (or any political party), he participated nevertheless in the alternative musical organizations and literary enterprises it supported. Among these were the Pierre Degeyter Club (named after the composer of the "Internationale"); the Composers' Collective, a spin-off group from the Degeyter Club; and the journals *New Masses* and *Music Vanguard*, published by the Workers' Music League, whose logo inter-twined its initials with a hammer and sickle, both set against a music staff. Copland marched along with thousands of other New Yorkers in May Day parades. Although he rarely attended the weekly meetings of the Composers' Collective, he performed in a concert of his music at the Degeyter Club in 1934. In 1933 the League inaugurated an annual festival called the Workers' Music

Ralph Steiner, Portrait of Aaron Copland. *Photograph, 1933.* © *Ralph Steiner Estate.*

Olympiad in the spring (near May Day), and in 1934 *New Masses* sponsored a competition for a "mass song" to be sung at the Second Annual American Workers' Music Olympiad in April. Copland entered and won this competition with his setting of Alfred Hayes's "Into the Streets May First!," a poem supplied by the Collective.[75] In 1935, Copland fulfilled a League of Composers commission with *Statements for Orchestra*, naming its six short movements with the political buzzwords of proletarian esthetics: "Militant," "Cryptic," "Dogmatic," "Subjective," "Jingo," and "Prophetic."[76]

What artistic impact did these volatile years have on Copland's music? With axioms like "national in form, proletarian in content" emerging from Party rhetoricians, Copland joined other composers like Marc Blitzstein, Earl Robinson, Henry Cowell, and Charles Seeger and his wife, Ruth Crawford, in trying to build bridges between their social conscience and their musical styles, seeking to reconcile their progressive (modernist) approach to their work with their progressive politics. Around 1932 Copland began to compose *Statements*, while Crawford wrote two declamatory songs of protest, "Sacco, Vanzetti" and "Chinaman, Laundryman," and Cowell wrote "Working Men Unite, We Must Put Up a Fight!" and "We Can Win Together."[77] The impassioned comrades explored ways to write mass songs in a progressive American idiom. Commercial (that is, capitalist-dominated) popular music would not do. Their credo insisted on a split between their work and Tin Pan Alley commercialism. They accompanied their militant protest lyrics in a style modeled after the workers' music that had been developed by Bertolt Brecht, Kurt Weill, and Hanns Eisler in Berlin. This idiom worked far better for Marc Blitztstein, whose memorable musical play *The Cradle Will Rock* (1937) came directly out of the Collective, than it did for Copland.[78]

Copland nevertheless made mass-song esthetics credible for himself. "Into the Streets May First!" has edgy militant rhythms, and its melody contains some daunting skips that need a complex harmony to complete them. A leader in the Composers' Collective, Charles Seeger (who took his young son, Pete—about ten years away from launching his career as a folk-revival singer—to May Day parades and Olympiads) once asked Copland, "Everybody here knows that your song is best. But do you think it will ever be sung on the picket line?" "No, I don't suppose it ever will be sung in a picket line," Copland responded.[79] Copland nonetheless gained experience in an idiom that would help him write the score for *The North Star*, a commercial film about Russia's battle against Germany made by Samuel Goldwyn in Hollywood in 1943. The didactic impulse, so essential to proletarian culture, surfaces in a number of the compositions Copland wrote at the intersection of art and politics during the 1930s.

To spread these ideas to a new generation, Copland composed a number of works for use in elementary and secondary schools, which he designed to introduce children to contemporary music and to advance politically progressive values. Both the choral piece "What Do We Plant?" and the piano piece "The Young Pioneers" evoke the mass song "Into the Streets May First!"[80] Fulfilling a commission from the Henry Street Settlement School on New York's Lower East Side, Copland wrote an opera, *The Second Hurricane*, which he modeled after the German *Lehrstück*, or didactic piece; the libretto emphasizes the virtues of collective action, in which disaster is averted by teamwork, "ev'rybody pulling together."[81] The values of cooperation and collective conscience should be seen not just as left-wing sectarianism but as part of the liberal consensus being forged under Roosevelt's New Deal. Although little known today, *The Second Hurricane* had enough impact to persuade the British composer Benjamin Britten to try his hand at the genre in his own children's opera, *Paul Bunyan*.

No matter how grim the times, Copland could still write to his good friend the Mexican composer Carlos Chávez that he was not "discouraged in any essential way."[82] Rather than brood over the lost avant-garde status of modernism and the demise of its patron class, Copland worked out a pragmatist esthetic. He explained his enlarged sense of responsibility in 1941 in an oft-quoted statement:

> During these years [early 1930s] I began to feel an increasing dissatisfaction with the relations of the music-loving public and the living composer. The old "special" public of the modern music concerts had fallen away, and the conventional concert public continued apathetic or indifferent to anything but the established classics. It seemed to me that we composers were in danger of working in a vacuum. Moreover, an entirely new public for music had grown up around the radio and phonograph. It made no sense to ignore them and to continue writing as if they did not exist.[83]

By 1940 Copland had fulfilled two commissions from the CBS Radio Broadcast Network, *Music for Radio* (1936; now known as *A Prairie Journal*) and an arrangement of the African-American blues ballad "John Henry" for the CBS School of the Air (1940). He also completed soundtracks for several films, among them a documentary, *The City* (1939), with a script by the reformist architectural writer Lewis Mumford, to celebrate the new, clean (and not so urban) city. Copland also completed scores for commercial films, among them *Of Mice and Men* (1939), based on John Steinbeck's 1937 novella, and *Our Town* (1940), based on Thornton Wilder's play. As one of the few classical composers to achieve success writing for Hollywood, he received multiple Academy Award nominations for his work. To extend the life of these scores beyond film, Copland recycled excerpts from them into independent concert suites, as with *Quiet City*, music intended for a play that was staged only in dress rehearsal.

Copland's influence on such genres as film and theater has yet to be fully appreciated. The nervous, lonely-crowd esthetic of *Quiet City* echoes in Leonard Bernstein's work. The domestic integrities of *Our Town* similarly resound in the score for the great postwar classic *The Best Years of Our Lives*, whose composer, Hugo Friedhofer, described Copland's practice of stripping bare the material in a new context: "The influence was largely in paring, in my weeding out the run-of-the-mill Hollywood schmaltz, and trying to do a very simple, straightforward, almost folklike score."[84] In his great ballets of the 1930s and 1940s Copland more deeply explored American folk music to address the changing American scene.

Grass Roots and Home-Front Culture

JUST AS JAZZ HAD INSPIRED ALLIANCES between classical and popular music in the 1920s, so folk music captured the imaginations of American composers in the late 1930s and 1940s. And just as jazz had spread across class and racial divides, by the 1940s folk music found its national middle-class urban audience, emerging from the first wave of what we now call the "urban folk-revival movement." The critic Paul Rosenfeld captured the change:

151

> A sensitiveness to the American folksong . . . on the part of the
> members of the urban and "educated" public was an event of
> the most recent years. It was said that, unlike Russia, France and
> Germany, the United States possessed no folk music. That of the
> Negro was quite simply "African." That of the mountaineers—
> one had the word of earlier ballad-collectors—was entirely
> Anglo-Celtic. The emergence into full view of the American
> folksong, if not the main musical event of the present, is its main
> American-musical one.[85]

Many factors contributed to this shift in taste. First, pioneering collectors like John and Alan Lomax, who shaped the holdings of the Archive of American Folk Song at the Library of Congress, documented the enormous creativity of the nation as a whole in such books as *American Ballads and Folk Songs* and *Our Singing Country*. What had been regarded only as regional or ethnic curiosities now emerged as national treasures. Second, by the late 1930s and early 1940s, advances in technology allowed folk-music collectors to produce "field recordings" from music they taped on site. The Archive of American Folk Song grew apace within the Library of Congress. Third, the imminent threat of a second world war made patriotism a political imperative, so that mobilizing on the home front involved culture as much as food rationing.

Folk music symbolized democracy made audible. In 1939, when the king and queen of England visited the Roosevelt White House, they heard cowboy songs performed by the folk-music collector Alan Lomax and Southern mountain music from the Coon Creek Girls of Kentucky. A few months later, the International Musicological Society, meeting in New York, sponsored concerts of Early American Folk-and-Art Music by the Nashville Old Harp Singers, and performances by Alan Lomax and, of Harlan County fame, Aunt Molly Jackson. "Quite a few composers turned out with high enthusiasm for the day's orgy of American folk music. The excitement with which some of them greet this music is in itself exciting to us," Ruth Crawford Seeger wrote to a colleague.[86] As Alan Lomax later recalled, "[what] we talked about all the time was how folk music could fertilize fine art music." In an article for *Modern Music* Charles Seeger exhorted American composers to get out into the field and discover their "grass roots."[87]

As with any coalescing trend, precedents abounded. In the late 1920s and mid-1930s, Virgil Thomson had pioneered the use of folk materials in both his *Symphony on a Hymn Tune* and in his famous film scores for the documentaries *The River* and *The Plow That Broke the Plains*. African-American composers like William Dawson and William Grant Still quoted spirituals in their symphonies. By the late 1930s and 1940s the trend that they had portended blossomed into full view. In conservatories across the country, classical music written by city-slicker composers included hoedowns, fuguing tunes, breakdowns, blues, cowboy ballads, lullabies, and spirituals. Into concert halls came such pieces as Roy Harris's *Folk Song Symphony*, Samuel Barber's piano arrangements of folk tunes, and Henry Cowell's *Hymn and Fuguing Tune*. Even Copland's French modernist hero, Darius Milhaud, having moved to the United States to escape the Nazis, composed *Kentuckiana*, an overture in the French style on twenty Kentucky airs.[88]

Copland traveled his own long, winding road into American tradition. He had already borrowed from both American and European vernacular music in many of his early pieces. Now he turned to the new collections of American songs that were published in the 1930s and 1940s. In his school opera *The Second Hurricane*, an Anglo-American folk tune from S. Foster Damon's *Old American Songs* (1936) appears at the penultimate moment, when the children sing a Revolutionary War song, "The Capture of Burgoyne." Borrowing other tunes from this collection later, Copland eventually used its title for two sets of very successful concert folk-song arrangements for solo voice and piano.[89] The tune "Springfield Mountain" turns up in Copland's work for speaker and orchestra, *Lincoln Portrait* (1942). In *Music for Radio*, Copland went beyond specific borrowing into a more generalized exploration of folk idiom by labeling the score for a pastoral theme for woodwinds "simply, in the manner of a folk song."

But how to do more? Copland had genuine reservations. He noted how the use of folk tunes "presents a formal problem when used in symphonic composition. Most composers have found that there is little that can be done with such material except repeat it."[90] In *El Salón México* he worked this through by subjecting several Mexican folk tunes to his kaleidoscopic approach from the 1920s, which he had demonstrated so successfully in *Music for the Theatre*. In depicting a "Popular Type Dance Hall in Mexico City," as he subtitled the work, Copland described his technique as a "modified potpourri in which the Mexican themes or fragments and extensions thereof are sometimes inextricably mixed."[91] He derived the tunes from two collections, Frances Toor's *Cancionero Mexicano* (1931, with illustrations by Rufino Tamayo) and Rubén Campos's *El Folklore y la Música Mexicana* (1928). For the climax Copland wove a polytonal fabric by presenting his borrowed tunes all at the same time, each in its own key. He colored the whole with dazzling orchestration that gives *El Salón México* its modernist sheen.

153

When Copland received a commission from a young American dance company, Ballet Caravan, for a score to a ballet that was to depict the life of the outlaw Billy the Kid, he pondered the use of folk materials once again. Hispanic tunes appealed to him more than what he initially disdained as "poverty-stricken" cowboy tunes.[92] In Paris for the summer of 1938, he perused several collections, among them *Songs of the Open Range* and *The Lonesome Cowboy: Songs of the Plains and Hills*, lent to him by Lincoln Kirstein, the director of the company. (Copland later said that he had taken these to Paris "in order to humor" Kirstein.)[93] And then the tunes lassoed him: "It wasn't very long before I found myself hopelessly involved in expanding, contracting, rearranging, and superimposing cowboy tunes on the rue de Rennes in Paris."[94]

Even so, *Billy the Kid* took a sharp turn on the road toward Copland's famous esthetic of plainness and simplicity. The most important compositions of the next decade, and indeed the some of the most influential of Copland's entire oeuvre, followed suit. Copland himself addressed the controversial issue of his esthetic shift several times, both privately and publicly, speaking, for example, about "a musical naturalness that we have badly needed—along with 'great' works."[95] He drew on folksy metaphors:

> As I look back, it seems to me that what I was trying for in the
> simpler works was only partly the writing of compositions that

might speak to a broader audience. More than that they gave me an opportunity to try for a more homespun musical idiom, not so different in intention from what attracted me in more hectic fashion in my jazz-influenced works of the twenties. In other words, it was not only musical functionalism that was in question, but also musical language.[96]

We can only highlight some of the most important strategies Copland employed in his "homespun musical idiom." With respect to folk melodies, he sometimes curbed his kaleidoscopic approach, spinning out folk songs for much longer, thus making them more easily recognizable. Frames of silence around such themes, or their equally ironic dismemberment into repeating motives, also create the illusion of a double-voiced discourse, the folk melody acting as one voice, and the composer's persona of objective urban narrator as another. Such techniques animate *Billy the Kid*'s largest scene, "Street in a Frontier Town," a medley of five tunes, with two pairs of tunes presented in counterpoint assigned to trotting

woodwinds. (Many later film composers turned to this section of the ballet as

George Platt Lynes, scene from Ballet Caravan production of Billy the Kid. *Photograph, gelatin silver print mounted on cardboard, 5 ⅞ x 4 ¾" (15 x 12 cm), 1938. Dance Division, The New York Public Library for the Performing Arts, Astor, Lenox, and Tilden Foundations.*

George Platt Lynes, scene from Ballet Caravan production of Billy the Kid. *Photograph, gelatin silver print mounted on cardboard, 5 ¹/₂ x 9 ¹/₄" (14 x 23.5 cm), 1938. Dance Division, The New York Public Library for the Performing Arts, Astor, Lenox, and Tilden Foundations.*

155

George Platt Lynes, scene from Ballet Caravan production of Billy the Kid. *Photograph, gelatin silver print mounted on cardboard, 7 ⁵/₈ x 7" (19.3 x 17.7 cm), 1938. Dance Division, The New York Public Library for the Performing Arts, Astor, Lenox, and Tilden Foundations.*

a way to write a Western sound.) In *Rodeo*'s third movement, "Saturday Night Waltz" transmutes a cowboy's sentimental farewell to his horse ("Goodbye Old Paint") into a tender love song, where rhythmically unpredictable accents in the harp that subvert the waltz meter also act as a delicate surrogate for a strumming guitar. Later in his career, after much more experience handling folk materials, Copland explained the way he worked:

> What, after all, does it mean to make use of a hymn tune or a cowboy tune in a serious musical composition? . . . The use of such materials ought never to be a mechanical process. They can be successfully handled only by a composer who is able to identify himself with, and reëxpress in his own terms, the underlying emotional connotation of the material. A hymn tune represents a certain order of feeling: simplicity, plainness, sincerity, directness. It is the reflection of those qualities in a stylistically appropriate setting, imaginative and unconventional and not mere quotation, that gives the use of folk tunes reality and importance.[97]

Copland's harmonic language makes the commonplace strange. The English critic Peter Evans describes how "Copland's hypersensitivity to chordal spacing and subtleties of instrumental distribution . . . give a new impact . . . to the common chord."[98] Thus, familiar diatonic chords (chords associated with one particular tonal center or key, such as those in the Christmas carol "Silent Night") often lack their sweetening interval (combination of two pitches), allowing leaner intervals such as fourths and fifths to twang away. Modal approaches (juxtaposing harmonies that would not be used in conventionally tonal music) flout conventional "voice-leading" rules of how one chord moves to the next. In *Billy the Kid*, the curtain rises on "The Open Prairie," depicted by streams of parallel fifths in the woodwinds that simultaneously paint a panoramic mural of a frontier processional as well as the stoicism that "Westering" (crossing the Western frontier) required.[99] In *Rodeo* the third dance begins with a startling extended gesture of upward-leaping fifths. Here Copland plays with the concert sound of a classical orchestra tuning up and, at the same time, the vernacular "discorded" tuning of rural Anglo-American fiddles, where the instrument's four strings are retuned to sound only one interval of a fifth. In the Lomax collection *Our Singing Country*, Copland learned about discorded tunings from the transcription of the fiddle tune "Bonyparte" (its name a variant of Bonaparte, for the piece describes Napoleon's army in battle). Copland turned discorded tuning into a fanfare, then swallowed the tune whole for the famous last movement of *Rodeo* now known as "Hoe-Down."

Affinities abound between Copland's esthetic of plainness and other kinds of American vernacular music. Just as folk art advocates like Holger Cahill stressed the compatibility of folk artifacts with modernist taste, some folk-music advocates found similar parallels in music. After George Pullen Jackson published *White Spirituals in the Southern Uplands* (1933), more urban American composers discovered the latent modernity in this repertory in particular. In 1936 Ruth Crawford Seeger prefaced her own piano arrangements of American folk tunes with the observation that traditional music from the southeastern United States "revels in these characteristics [lean, spare harmonies and unconventional tonal practice] of modern music."[100] A few years later her husband, Charles, explicitly connected the "music puritanism" of rural American hymn writers to the "music puritanism" of the French modernist composer Erik Satie.[101] Copland, who encountered rural hymnody in S. Foster Damon's *Old American Songs*, and later used other tunes from Pullen Jackson's collections, described the well-known nineteenth-century rural hymn book *The Sacred Harp* as "American folk-art."[102] Putting such idioms to use in *Fanfare for the Common Man*, Copland used diatonic fourths and fifths with a jagged, wide-ranging melody to produce a deceptive ruggedness, writing a modernist version of the American military bugle call taps. Buried beneath the brassy assertiveness of *Fanfare* is the spiritual directness of hymnody.

That Copland did not have to quote folk tunes directly to employ his "homespun" idiom testifies to its musical autonomy. The music he wrote for the film *Our Town*, for example, avoids the specificity of an American folk tune in order to stress the universality of Wilder's homage to everyday life. The composer and critic Arthur Berger writes eloquently of the "restrained, beatific New England sorrow" in Copland's score.[103] The *Sonata for Violin and Piano* (1943) is another case in point. As Copland recalled later, "For whatever reasons, at that time I had little desire to compose a dissonant or virtuosic work, or one that incorporated folk materials. Nevertheless, certain qualities of the American folk tune had become part of my natural style of composing, and they are echoed in the *Sonata*."[104] Those "certain qualities" (most characteristic of Anglo-American rather than African-American folk music) were the consonant brightness of the tunes and their spare melodic lines often shaped by leaping intervals of their common chords. That Copland acknowledged his internalization of this idiom so matter-of-factly testifies to the bond between his own temperament and American vernacular. His friend the composer Israel Citkowitz wrote insightfully about this: "In creating a new center of responsibility for himself, there was no trace of condescension, but an attitude, instead, of complete identification. . . . It engaged his sensibilities to a degree that was not suspected at the time."[105]

157

Such identification enabled a dialogue between tradition and modernity in Copland's music. His work with folk materials enriched his experimental approach to how musical time might be shaped as he ventured ever deeper into his own minimalist world. His radical practice was shaped by a paradox, in that the most basic materials of conventional harmony bonded with his experiments in modernist immobility. Particularly in the slow sections of various compositions, an idiom of harmonic stasis (where chords do not "progress" through key centers) is associated with a mood that magnifies tranquility into meditation. The famous opening vista of *Appalachian Spring*, built on the three most common chords in tonal language, is one of the miracles of Copland's oeuvre. Described by Martha Graham in an early script for the ballet, it is supposed to coordinate with the character of the Mother, who "looks out over the land she has helped to stake and claim and win."[106]

As much as this music looks out, so does the *Piano Sonata* look in. Its last movement contains the paradox of the most skeletonized music conveying psychological mysteries. Commenting on this work, Copland's friend Harold Clurman told him: "I think about your sonata a lot. About its meaning in relation to you. . . . I find things in your Sonata—deeply buried things. . . . You are in a way like the traditional 'Englishman,' simple, practical, well adjusted on the outside with a whole other world inside that has to be guessed at but is never articulated—save in idiosyncrasies or works of art."[107] There is an aura of asceticism about this movement: stark, repeated chord patterns framed by silence, the dotted motives that outline simple intervals over and over, the sustained tones in the left-hand bass and the thumb of the right hand, which then leaps up into bare skips. No counterpoint softens the gonglike dissonances in the middle section. The final moments, marked "elegiac," rely on only two notes at a time, played amid the resonance of pedal points to accompany the composer's withdrawal into mystery and solitude. Is this the ultimate consequence of vernacular simplicity? The astute British critic Wilfrid Mellers describes this as the "quintessential expression of immobility."[108] "[That] seems to say in prose what I had in mind when I was composing the music," Copland said later.[109]

In the 1930s and 1940s Copland continued to collaborate with innovative American choreographers who made that era a golden age of modern dance. In his ballets Copland thrived on the creative minds that allowed him the musical opportunities to give full range to his plangent wistfulness, his tender objectivity, his ironic heroic gestures of masculinity, and his desolate lyricism. To some extent, the specific musical style he adopted for each of the ballets he scored reflects the temperaments of the choreographers involved. In *Billy the Kid*, Eugene Loring turned an outlaw into a misunderstood adolescent and, drawing on his own homosexual sensibility, intensified the homoerotic potential in the separatist world of range-roving men. In *Rodeo*, the feisty choreographer Agnes de Mille made the protagonist of her cowboy community a brash young innocent woman standing at the threshold of love, whose desire initiates a battle of the sexes. (She would exploit this theme later in her choreography for the musical *Oklahoma!*) In *Appalachian Spring*, while Martha Graham provided a psychodrama that acted as an astringent choreographic counterpoint to Copland's score (in fact, the original ballet score has moments of darkness—later excised from Copland's adapted ballet suite—that emphasize the Graham psychology even more), Copland stated that it was

> her personal manner that inspired the style of the music. Martha is rather prim and restrained, simple, yet strong, and her dance style is correspondingly direct. One thinks of these qualities as being especially American, and thus, the character of my score, which quotes only one actual folk tune . . . uses rhythms, harmonies and melodies that suggest an American ambience.[110]

159

What was that American "ambience?" The question takes on particular resonance with respect to this ballet, most of which Copland wrote with a different scenario in mind. He loved to tell the story of how the title *Appalachian Spring* came to Graham after the ballet was completed, thus foiling those listeners who heard a nature painting in every turn of phrase. He also knew that he had recycled sections from his incidental music *Quiet City* into this ballet. Nevertheless, certain elements remained consistent during the strange journey of Graham's story line. From start to finish Copland knew "that it had to do with the pioneer American spirit, with youth and spring, with optimism and hope."[111] And: "Even when the script was in its early stages, Martha had envisioned 'a new town, someplace where the first fence has just gone up . . . the framework of a doorway, the platform of a porch, a Shaker rocking chair with its exquisite bonelike simplicity, and a small fence that should signify what a fence means in a new country.'"[112] Perhaps this imagery led Copland to the Shaker tune "Simple Gifts," with its famous set of variations serving as the climax for the ballet. Such imagery went hand in hand with still pervasive, deeply cherished beliefs about American national character. Graham translated into dance our ideologies of settler culture: The pristine wilderness, which releases us from the suffocations of the Old World, is domesticated; our settlers embody self-reliance and community responsibility; they (and we) read the vastness of American land as our potential and its open air as our innocence.

Thus, no matter what the particulars of plot in any of Copland's ballets, a dramatic character common to all of them is landscape. In *Rodeo*, Agnes de

Mille instructed Copland that "one must be always conscious of the enormous land on which these people live and of their proud loneliness."[113] In *Appalachian Spring*, Graham's dancers responded to the impact of his idiom:

> The idea of space is like fuel to a dancer. Aaron has given sound to this space. . . . We thank Aaron for the wide use of time that his music provides, for the energy his music ignites in us, and for the limitless space that we hear in his sound. With Aaron's music, one leaps not across the stage, but across the land.[114]

In an emergent country like ours, where we have created, for better and worse, an ideology of geography to explain our history as colonials who colonize, the idea of space fuses with destiny. Where do we come from? Where are we going? In an emergent culture for indigenous classical music, Copland asked, can music and the life around us touch? As he transmuted identity-through-landscape into landscape-within-music, Copland answered questions through metaphors of place that allow us to experience multiple and contradictory truths at once.

Cold War Modern

"GOD *damn* SIMPLICITY!" Charles Ives once exclaimed to the pianist John Kirkpatrick, who had "innocently spoken the word [simplicity] by which the new generation [of the 1930s–1940s] condemned Ives's music."[115] (At least so Ives believed.) Simplicity and landscape continue to resonate in some of Copland's best work in the last decades of his life. In describing *Old American Songs* (1950–1952), the biographer Howard Pollack points to the "stunning river landscape" in "The Boatmen's Dance" and the "full-scale tone painting in 'The Golden Willow Tree.'"[116] In another song from this set, the rural Southern hymn "Zion's Walls," the vibrant dancing rhythms of the tune make a congregation trip the light fantastic. Both the tune "Zion's Walls" and the countermelody Copland composed for it became the basis of the great quintet finale to act 1 of his opera *The Tender Land* (1954). There, a hymn to Jesus is transformed into a "harvest home chorale," to borrow a title from Ives himself.[117]

After World War II, when the lay of the land looked different to Americans as they stared across oceans at new allies and new enemies, it was Copland's turn to have his own stylistic priorities interrogated. During the spring of 1949, visiting Europe for the first time in twelve years, Copland met with Pierre Boulez, the ambitious leader of the French post–World War II avant-garde who, in 1945, had led a demonstration against Stravinsky's neoclassical chamber suite *Danses Concertantes* at its European premiere in Paris.[118] Copland said, "Well, I know Boulez didn't like my music, but since I managed to walk up those four floors, he treated me with respect."[119] What Boulez did like was the controlled magic of Anton Webern's "twelve-tone," or "serial," music. (Serial composition means the organization of the twelve pitches of the Western scale into a series or row, and the subsequent derivation of an entire piece based on manipulations of the row.) Boulez was not alone, as a new generation of Western classical composers, crossing the boundaries of Germany and France as well as the Atlantic Ocean, rejected the populist esthetics of the World War II era and rededicated themselves to the musical priorities of a prewar avant-garde. From the late 1940s throughout the next two decades, such figures as Boulez in France and Milton Babbitt in the United States reconstructed new music on the techniques pioneered in the music of what is called the Second Viennese School—the radical atonality and serial techniques initiated by Arnold Schoenberg and later disseminated through the influential works of his two famous students, Webern and Alban Berg.

Fifty years of age at midcentury, even from his position as a composer of great stature, Copland felt pressure from a younger generation that was eager to put out to pasture his essentially tonal approach to music. By the early 1950s he essayed his first compositions using serial techniques in such compositions as the *Piano Quartet* (1950), and then continued to use the method in two late orchestral works, *Connotations* (1962) and *Inscape* (1967). Some critics reacted as if Copland had converted to a new religion, and treated these works as apostate music. Copland explained that he was looking for ways to "freshen and enrich my technique." "I need more chords," he told Leonard Bernstein. "I've run out of chords." He used serial approaches as a way to invent them.[120]

Even so, Copland remained a nonsystematist at a time when theoretical approaches stressing premeditative compositional strategies began their climb up the prestige ladder. Asked to give the important Charles Eliot Norton Lectures at Harvard in the 1950–1951 academic year, Copland spoke passionately about his subject, music and imagination. (The lectures were subsequently published under this title as Copland's third book.) During an era when scientific paradigms dominated intellectual musical discourse among white classical composers, it took some courage to make pronouncements like this:

> My own mind feels more at home with the unsystematic approach
> of writers like Montaigne and Goethe, let us say; and especially in
> the field of music it seems to me important that we keep open what
> William James calls the "irrational doorways . . . through which the
> wildness and pang of life" may be glimpsed.[121]

In so many ways Copland walked through those Jamesian doorways in the last decades of his life. Certainly the extent to which he had to cope with an early decline of both his creative and mental powers afforded him glimpses of life's pang. His output slowed in the 1960s. The plague of memory decline hit him in his mid-seventies, foreshadowing the senility that became increasingly pronounced in the 1980s. By the early 1970s Copland admitted to friends that he no longer felt driven to compose, and he turned all of his musicianship toward conducting.

Nevertheless, Copland's sense of place as a key to his musical personality continued to loom just as large during these years as it had previously. Looking backward at his creative output, Copland said, "The idea of a 'scape' of any kind—a landscape, or an inscape, or an escape—seemed to lend itself in a general way to a music piece because it is so general."[122] His music suggests all these vistas, as indicated even externally by their titles and sometimes his own comments in and around the scores. Of the *Piano Fantasy* (1957) Copland wrote that he wanted the form to suggest "a spontaneous and unpremeditated sequence of 'events,'" underscoring emphatically the illusion of irrational play at its core;[123] he even considered naming it "The Music Within." Copland's exploration of "within" marked off the boundaries of his musical imagination so acutely that he named his last orchestral work *Inscape*. Here he borrowed a word coined by the poet Gerard Manley Hopkins to mean the Platonic essential qualities of things. Even that most celebratory of forms, the fanfare, evoked meditative responses from Copland in his late sixties. The *Inaugural Fanfare* (1969), commissioned by the city of Grand Rapids, Michigan, in honor of the installation of an Alexander Calder stabile, contains a surprisingly plaintive middle section for two trumpets, where the two horns reiterate the opening theme (full of characteristic Copland leaps) against an improvising snare drum. Similarly, a commission from the Van Cliburn Foundation for a piano work to be used in its celebrated competition drew from Copland not a virtuoso display piece, but rather, one of the most idiosyncratic works he ever wrote: *Night Thoughts* (1972), subtitled *Homage to Ives*. Copland explained the rationale behind his nocturne as a way "to test the musicality and ability of the performer to give coherence to a free musical form."[124]

Most critics of Copland's oeuvre do not believe his late work sustains the level of achievement of his middle-period music, particularly that of his ballets. Yet for many, the compositions Copland wrote after 1950, in spite of their flaws, confirm his vital musical imagination still at work. In *Night Thoughts*, for example, while a three-note motive does unify the work as a whole, the material does not support the kind of emotional energy Copland evidently believed the piece contained. Not much lyricism envelops the bare linear passage marked "simply singing"; nor does the passage marked "eloquently" support that wish either. Instead, obsessive reiterations of chords and piano figurations, ranging over the extremes of the piano, are repeated over and over again. This suggests Copland's own inner preoccupations, perhaps with decline and death.

Thus the piece projects a haunting atmosphere of private contemplative candor, as if clues to the beyond could be found in overtones; it is an old man's work. With respect to Copland's last orchestral works, *Inscape* and, most certainly, its earlier sister-piece, *Connotations*, both contain massive chordal assaults on the ear, intensified by brittle orchestral timbres. According to Copland, *Connotations* depicted the harshness of modern urban existence. But above and beyond any particulars of cityscapes in that work or the elemental essence of *Inscape*, Copland's acknowledgment of the darkness revealed in such early works from the 1920s as the *Symphonic Ode* and *Piano Variations* comes to the forefront of his artistic consciousness once again at this point in his career. These late works contain some of the most dissonant, abrasive chords he ever wrote. How often his ear gives us harmonies that speak John Donne's words: "Never send to know for whom the bell tolls; It tolls for thee."

Although no final judgment can yet be passed on Copland's late music, many believe that his outstanding contribution from 1950 onward was his collaboration with a kindred spirit, one who gave him the best literary material of any of his text-based compositions: the poet Emily Dickinson. Like so many other of his works, Copland's song cycle *Twelve Poems of Emily Dickinson* (1950) initially received a lukewarm reception, entering into the concert repertory only slowly. Nevertheless, the affinity between two ascetic minds—the mid-nineteenth-century recluse whose art honed vernacular speech into razor-sharp imagery, and a composer who distilled folk idioms into a minimalist style—proved salutary. Copland explained his choice of twelve poems from the more than one thousand that Dickinson wrote: "The poems center about no single theme, but they treat of a subject matter particularly close to Miss Dickinson: nature, death, life, eternity."[125] In contrast to the reconciling visions of nature Copland composed for his 1940s ballets, here he confronted Dickinson's radical tragedies. As the critic Guy Rotella has written, "Dickinson's experiment with nature discovered darkness at noon. The world was inscribed with God's truth; the truth was a horror."[126] Meeting Dickinson's challenge of subversive spirituality, Copland employed the same kind of radical diatonic harmony he used for the *Piano Sonata*, as well as other idioms from his past: bitonal mergers, gonglike pedals, skeletal dissonances, and, of course, simple major triads. In contrast to much earlier work, notable for its neglect of counterpoint, here the piano writing is more linear than chordal, behaving like a partner in a metaphysical dialogue.

The composer felt equal to the poet, meeting her across a gender divide that meant little to him. He wrote the songs for a female voice, questioning whether or not a male voice could do them justice. After all, they were written by a female poet and composed, as he once said, "from a woman's point of view."[127] Did they not both share what the feminist Elizabeth Cady Stanton called "the solitude of self"?

163

While working on his Dickinson settings Copland visited the poet's house in Amherst, Massachusetts. He walked upstairs to her bedroom "to see what she saw out of that window." What was her street like? Copland noted the green view from her room, which allowed her to see "the main crossroads of the town." His imagination quickened at the contrast between Dickinson's passionate inscape and the peopled world experienced mainly through a few panes of glass. How far he himself had traveled beyond his "drab street in Brooklyn." As befitted a man who searched for ways to make music and life meet, where Emily Dickinson lived filled Copland with mild wonder.[128] Who ever would have associated such poetry with that place?

NOTES

Aaron Copland's America

Gail Levin

1. Aaron Copland to Vivian Perlis, interview transcript (interviews taped 1975–1976), box 226/5, p. 73, Library of Congress, Copland Collection [hereafter CCLC].
2. Copland to Perlis, interview transcript, box 226/5, p. 106, CCLC.
3. Copland to Perlis, interview transcript, box 226/5, p. 105, CCLC.
4. Aaron Copland, "The Composer in Industrial America," in *Music and Imagination* (Cambridge: Harvard University Press, 1952), p. 106.
5. Max Weber, *Cubist Poems* (London: Elkin Mathews, 1914). Alvin Langdon Coburn, who wrote the introduction to the book, remarked on his friend's sympathy for Picasso's painting. Weber's last show with Stieglitz, with whom he had a falling out, was in 1911.
6. Aaron Copland, WPA Composers' Forum-Laboratory, New York City, February 24, 1937, *WPA Composers* [sic] *Forum Transcripts*, National Archives, as quoted in Barbara A. Zuck, *A History of Musical Americanism* (Ann Arbor, Mich.: UMI Research Press, 1980), p. 251.
7. Carol Oja, "Women Patrons and Crusaders for Modernist Music: New York in the 1920s," in Ralph P. Locke and Cyrilla Barr, eds., *Cultivating Music in America: Women Patrons and Activists Since 1860* (Berkeley: University of California Press, 1997), p. 265. This reception was held in New York after one of the concerts in the series presented by Copland and his fellow composer Roger Sessions from 1928 through 1931.
8. For Copland's own account of his life and memoirs of various friends and associates, see Aaron Copland and Vivian Perlis, *Copland 1900 Through 1942* (New York: St. Martin's Press, 1984), and Aaron Copland and Vivian Perlis, *Copland Since 1943* (New York: St. Martin's Press, 1989). For a more comprehensive biographical overview and analysis, as well as a useful selected bibliography, see Howard Pollack, *Aaron Copland: The Life and Work of an Uncommon Man* (New York: Henry Holt, 1999).
9. Copland and Perlis, *Copland 1900 Through 1942*, p. 17.
10. Copland and Perlis, *Copland 1900 Through 1942*, p. 32.
11. Program for Leo Ornstein concert, captioned "Last New York Recital," November 29, 1919, 3:00 o'clock, Aeolian Hall, 34 West 43d Steet, New York; this document is on file in the Music Division of The New York Public Library.
12. Frederick H. Martens, *Leo Ornstein the Man—His Ideas, His Work* (New York: Breitkopf & Hartel, 1918), p. 62.
13. See Gail Levin, "Kandinsky's Debut in America," in Gail Levin and Marianne Lorenz, *Theme & Improvisation: Kandinsky & the American Avant-Garde, 1912–1950* (Boston: Bulfinch Press, 1992), pp. 10–11.

14. Hippolyte Havel, *Camera Work*, no. 47 (dated July 1914, published January 1915): 67.
15. See Paul Avrich, *The Modern School Movement: Anarchism and Education in the United States* (Princeton, N.J.: Princeton University Press, 1980).
16. Colin Rhodes, *Primitivism and Modern Art* (London: Thames & Hudson, 1994), p. 13.
17. Martens, *Leo Ornstein*, p. 64.
18. Rosenfeld quoted in Martens, *Leo Ornstein*, pp. 51 and 66, the latter referring to Ornstein's first *Impression de Notre Dame*.
19. The *Pygmy Suite op. 9* is not included in the "Selective List of Works" in the entry on Ornstein by Vivian Perlis in H. Wiley Hitchcock and Stanley Sadie, eds., *The New Grove Dictionary of American Music* (New York and London: Macmillan, 1986), 3:452. This work appears in the catalogue of The New York Public Library as Leo Ornstein, *Pygmy Suite; Eight Pieces for the Pianoforte, Op. 9* (Boston: Boston Music Co., c. 1914); the contents are listed as "Serenade," "Hunting Song," "Berceuse," "The Dance," "Evening Prayer," "March," "By the Brook," and "Merry-making." Martens, *Leo Ornstein*, p. 60, also refers to this work, calling it *Pigmy Suite, Op. 9*; an advertisement at the end of this book, on p. 90, lists "Pygmy Suite Op. 9" as a "Piano Solo."
20. See Gail Levin, "'Primitivism' in American Art: Some Literary Parallels of the 1910s and 1920s," *Arts Magazine* 59, no. 3:101–105, and Gail Levin, "American Art," in William Rubin, ed., *"Primitivism" in 20th Century Art: Affinity of the Tribal and the Modern* (New York: Museum of Modern Art, 1984), 2:452–473. See also Helen M. Shannon, "American Modernist Primitivism: Cultural Nationalism, Race, and the Perception of African Art, 1914–1934" (Ph.D. diss., Columbia University, 1999), p. 70, note 20; and Kathy J. Ogren, *The Jazz Revolution: Twenties America and the Meaning of Jazz* (New York: Oxford University Press, 1989). This last reference goes much beyond the scope of my *Arts Magazine* article to explore primitivism in the debate about jazz.
21. Copland and Perlis, *Copland 1900 Through 1942*, pp. 124–125.
22. See Alan Trachtenberg, ed., *Memoirs of Waldo Frank* (Amherst, Mass.: University of Massachusetts Press, 1973), pp. 83–95.
23. Paul Rosenfeld, "The American Composer," *The Seven Arts* 1 (November 1916): 89.
24. Copland and Perlis, *Copland 1900 Through 1942*, p. 125.
25. Waldo Frank, *Our America* (New York: Boni & Liveright, 1919), p. 187.
26. Frank, *Our America*, p. 188.
27. Frank, *Our America*, pp. 184, 230.
28. Copland and Perlis, *Copland 1900 Through 1942*, p. 28.

29. Walt Whitman, "I Hear America Singing," in Maxwell Geismar, ed., *The Whitman Reader* (New York: Pocket Books, 1955), p. 5.

30. James Oppenheim, "Poetry—Our First National Art," in William Wasserstrom, ed., *A Dial Miscellany* (Syracuse, N.Y.: Syracuse University Press, 1963), p. 3.

31. See Nicholas Joost, *Scofield Thayer and* The Dial: *An Illustrated History* (Carbondale, Ill.: Southern Illinois University Press, 1964), p. 1.

32. See Wasserstrom, *A Dial Miscellany*, p. xx.

33. Daniel Catton Rich, "Dial M for Modern," *The Dial and The Dial Collection* (Worcester, Mass.: Worcester Art Museum, 1959), p. 7.

34. Copland to his parents, letters of June 22, 1921, and December 4, 1921, CCLC.

35. Copland to his parents, letter of June 10, 1921, CCLC; quoted in Copland and Perlis, *Copland 1900 Through 1942*, p. 42.

36. Copland and Perlis, *Copland 1900 Through 1942*, p. 44.

37. Copland to Perlis, interview transcript, box 226/5, pp. 73, 75, CCLC. On Duchamp, see Calvin Tomkins, *Duchamp: A Biography* (New York: Henry Holt, 1996), pp. 12, 210–211.

38. Copland to his parents, letter of June 18, 1921, CCLC.

39. Copland to his parents, letter of June 22, 1921, CCLC.

40. Copland and Perlis, *Copland 1900 Through 1942*, pp. 44–45.

41. Copland to his parents, letter of November 3, 1921, CCLC.

42. Harold Clurman, *All People Are Famous (Instead of an Autobiography)* (New York: Harcourt Brace Jovanovich, 1974), p. 65.

43. Clurman, *All People Are Famous*, p. 66.

44. See Michel Sanouillet and Elmer Peterson, *The Essential Writings of Marcel Duchamp* (London: Thames & Hudson, 1975), pp. 24, 35, 109. See also Gavin Bryars, "Notes on Marcel Duchamp's Music," *Studio International* 984 (1976): 274–279, and Carol P. James, "Duchamp's Silent Music/Music for the Deaf," in Rudolf E. Kuenzli and Francis M. Naumann, *Marcel Duchamp: Artist of the Century* (Cambridge: MIT Press, 1990), p. 113. John Cage later recorded Duchamp's *Musical Erratum* for the Paula Cooper Gallery, New York.

45. Sanouillet and Peterson, *Duchamp*, p. 75.

46. Copland and Perlis, *Copland 1900 Through 1942*, p. 44. According to Copland to Perlis, interview transcript, box 226/5, p. 77, CCLC, he also saw *L'Homme et Son Désir* with music by Darius Milhaud. *Les Mariés de la Tour Eiffel* premiered on June 18, 1921, and *L'Homme et Son Désir* opened June 6, 1921.

47. Copland to his parents, letter of August 3, 1921, CCLC.

48. Clurman quoted in Copland and Perlis, *Copland 1900 Through 1942*, p. 57.

49. Clurman to Louis Shaeffer, "Reminiscences: An Oral History," in Marjorie Loggia and Glenn Young, eds., *The Collected Works of Harold Clurman* (New York: Applause Theatre Pubs., 1994), p. 958.

50. Clurman, *All People Are Famous*, p. 30.

51. Copland and Perlis, *Copland 1900 Through 1942*, p. 56.

52. André Breton, "Silence Is Golden," *Modern Music* 21, no. 3 (March–April 1944). André Breton's book *Situation du Surréalisme entre les Deux Guerres* (Paris: Éditions de la Révue Fontaine, 1945) is now in the Copland Collection at the Library of Congress. Although some art books from Copland's personal library remain today in his house in Cortlandt, New York, others were dispersed according to his will, in which he invited a group of his friends to choose various books. No list of these items has yet come to light.

53. Copland to his parents, unpublished letter of June 24, 1921, CCLC.

54. Matthew Josephson, "The Great American Billposter," *Broom* 3 (November 1922): 305.

55. James Weldon Johnson, *Along the Way: The Autobiography of James Weldon Johnson* (1933; reprint, New York: Viking Press, 1968), pp. 172–173, recalls going to Marshall's. See also Eileen Southern and Josephine Wright, comps., *African-American Traditions in Song, Sermon, Tale, and Dance, 1600s–1920: An Annotated Bibliography of Literature, Collections, and Artworks* (Westport, Conn.: Greenwood Press, 1990), p. 265.

56. Duchamp interview, January 21, 1956, by Emily Farnham in *Charles Demuth: Behind a Laughing Mask* (Norman, Okla.: University of Oklahoma Press, 1971), p. 103.

57. John Marin to Alfred Stieglitz, letter of September 24, 1924, Stonington, Maine; quoted in Ruth E. Fine, *John Marin* (New York: Abbeville Press, 1990), p. 145, and Dorothy Norman, ed., *The Selected Writings of John Marin* (New York: Pellegrini & Cudahy, 1949), p. 100.

58. This ballet was first performed in New York on November 26, 1923. See Gail Levin, "The Ballets Suédois and American Culture," in Nancy Van Norman Baer, ed., *Paris Modern: The Swedish Ballet, 1920–1925* (San Francisco: Fine Arts Museums of San Francisco, 1996), p. 124.

59. Alfred Kreymborg, *Troubadour: An Autobiography* (New York: Liveright, 1925), p. 366.

60. Levin, "The Ballets Suédois and American Culture," pp. 118–127. Sara Murphy, Gerald's wife, may have designed these costumes.

61. Aaron Copland, "Music Between the Wars (1918–1939)" in *The New Music: 1900–1960* (New York: W. W. Norton, 1968), p. 61. See also Glenn Watkins, *Pyramids at the Louvre: Music, Culture, and Collage from Stravinsky to the Postmodernists* (Cambridge: Harvard University Press, 1994), pp. 115–116.

62. Copland, "Music Between the Wars," p. 61.

63. See Copland, "Composer from Brooklyn: An Autobiographical Sketch," in *The New Music*, p. 151. Neil Butterworth, *The Music of Aaron Copland* (New York: Universe Books, 1985), p. 17, and Arthur Berger, *Aaron Copland* (New York: Oxford University Press, 1953; reprint, Westport, Conn.: Greenwood Press, 1976), p. 3.

64. Igor Stravinsky, *Ragtime* (Paris: Éditions de la Sirène, 1919).

65. Copland and Perlis, *Copland 1900 Through 1942*, p. 72.

66. Minna Lederman, *The Life and Death of a Small Magazine: Modern Music, 1924–1946* (Brooklyn, N.Y.: ISAM, 1983), p. 3. Stephan Bourgeois, the New York art dealer who was on the board of the League of Composers, obtained permission from Picasso to reproduce these drawings, as well as two others that Picasso had made of Erik Satie and Manuel De Falla. *Modern Music* was originally titled *The League of Composers' Review*.

67. Copland and Perlis, *Copland 1900 Through 1942*, p. 73.

68. Copland, "The Composer in Industrial America," p. 99.

69. Copland, "The Composer in Industrial America," pp. 99–100.

70. Arnold Dobrin, *Aaron Copland: His Life and Times* (New York: Thomas Y. Crowell, 1967), p. 61.

71. Copland and Perlis, *Copland 1900 Through 1942*, pp. 101–102.

72. Copland to Perlis, interview transcript, box 226/4, p. 2, CCLC; Perlis omitted this comment from the book.

73. Copland and Perlis, *Copland 1900 Through 1942*, p. 102.

74. Hart Crane to Grace Hart Crane, letter of November 30, 1924, in Thomas S. W. Lewis, *Letters of Hart Crane and His Family* (New York: Columbia University Press, 1974), p. 378. Lewis incorrectly identified "Seligman" as the New York art dealer Jacques Seligman, but it was surely Herbert J. Seligmann, a writer, editor, and Stieglitz intimate, who was present.

75. Edmund Wilson quoted in Charles Norman, *E. E. Cummings: The Magic-Maker* (New York: Macmillan, 1958), pp. 141–142.

76. Ezra Pound, "Immorality," in *Ripostes* (London: Stephen Swift, 1912), p. 192. Copland and Perlis, *Copland 1900 Through 1942*, p. 116, identified Pound's poem incorrectly as a text from *Lustra* of 1916.

77. Copland and Perlis, *Copland 1900 Through 1942*, p. 120.

78. Bernard Sobel, *A Pictorial History of Burlesque* (New York: Bonanza Books, 1956), pp. 172–173.

79. Copland and Perlis, *Copland 1900 Through 1942*, p. 119.

80. Copland and Perlis, *Copland 1900 Through 1942*, p. 134.

81. Copland and Perlis, *Copland 1900 Through 1942*, p. 119.

82. For a discussion of other contemporary attitudes toward jazz, many of them less progressive than Copland's, see Ogren, *The Jazz Revolution*, pp. 151–161.

83. Paul Rosenfeld, "Jazz and Music: Music in America," *An Hour with American Music* (Philadelphia: J. B. Lippincott, 1929), p. 11.

84. F. Scott Fitzgerald, "Echoes of the Jazz Age," *Scribner's Magazine* (November 1931), quoted in Malcom Cowley and Robert Cowley, *Fitzgerald and the Jazz Age* (New York: Charles Scribner's Sons, 1966), pp. 125–183. In a letter he wrote to his editor, Maxwell Perkins, in May 1931, Fitzgerald claimed to have coined this phrase. The letter is reprinted in Andrew Turnbull, ed., *The Letters of F. Scott Fitzgerald* (New York: Charles Scribner's Sons, 1963), p. 225.

85. Hart Crane to Allen Tate, letter of May 16, 1922, in Brom Weber, ed., *The Letters of Hart Crane, 1916–1932* (New York: Hermitage House, 1952; paperback reprint, Berkeley: University of California Press, 1965), p. 89.

86. Herbert Leibowitz, *Hart Crane: An Introduction to the Poetry* (New York: Columbia University Press, 1968), p. 238.

87. Hart Crane to Grace Hart Crane, letter of November 30, 1924, in Lewis, *Letters of Hart Crane and His Family*, pp. 377–378.

88. Arnold Rampersad, ed., *The Collected Poems of Langston Hughes* (New York: Alfred A. Knopf, 1994), p. 60.

89. Paul Mariani, *William Carlos Williams: A New World Naked* (New York: McGraw-Hill, 1981), p. 513.

90. Carl Van Vechten, "Pastiches et Pistaches," *The Reviewer* 2, no. 4 (February 1922): 270.

91. Van Vechten, "Pastiches," p. 270.

92. Clurman in *The Collected Works*, p. 98.

93. Barbara J. Bloemink, *The Life and Art of Florine Stettheimer* (New Haven: Yale University Press, 1995), p. 155.

94. It is currently in the collection of the Museum of the City of New York.

95. For an account of one dinner at which Copland was present, see Steven Watson, *Prepare for Saints: Gertrude Stein, Virgil Thomson, and the Mainstreaming of American Modernism* (New York: Random House, 1998), pp. 71–72.

96. Zuck, *A History of Musical Americanism*, p. 263.

97. Copland and Perlis, *Copland 1900 Through 1942*, p. 75.

98. Virgil Thomson, "Aaron Copland," *Modern Music* 9, no. 2 (January–February 1932): 67. In fact, Copland and Thomson wrote about each other's music; Thomson reviewed Copland's book *Our New Music* (New York: McGraw-Hill, 1941), which was later revised and expanded as *The New Music*.

99. Virgil Thomson, in Barbara Zuck, ed., "Virgil Thomson: American Music and Music Criticism," *The Otterbein Miscellany* 12, no. 1 (December 1976): 18. Virgil Thomson, *American Music Since 1910* (New York: Holt, Rinehart & Winston, 1972), p. 55.

100. Maldwyn Allen Jones, *American Immigration* (Chicago: University of Chicago Press, 1960), pp. 276–277. The racist quota excluded all but a few countries from Western Europe; this is the quota referred to in Gerald Murphy and Cole Porter's 1923 ballet *Within the Quota*.

101. Forbes Watson, "The All American Nineteen," *The Arts* 16 (January 1930): 308–310.

102. Julia Frances Smith, "Aaron Copland, His Work and Contribution to American Music" (Ph.D. diss., New York University, 1952), p. 164.

103. See Standish D. Lawder, *The Cubist Cinema* (New York: New York University Press, 1975), pp. 117–118; Linda Whitesitt, *The Life and Music of George Antheil, 1900–1959* (Ann Arbor, Mich.: UMI Research Press, 1981), pp. 106–107.

104. Copland and Perlis, *Copland 1900 Through 1942*, p. 127. The letter was to the composer Israel Citkowitz.

105. Copland and Perlis, *Copland 1900 Through 1942*, p. 127. Aaron Copland, "George Antheil," *League of Composers' Review* 2, no. 1 (January 1925): 26.

106. Copland, "George Antheil," p. 26.

107. George Antheil to *Modern Music* (1925), reprinted in Lederman, *Small Magazine*, p. 16.

108. See *This Quarter* 1, no. 2 (Milan, Italy: 1925). This issue, which featured a supplement with extracts from Antheil's music, also contained prose as well as poems by Ezra Pound, Carl Sandburg, and others.

109. Antheil to Copland, letter of June 16, 1933, CCLC.

110. Antheil to Copland, letter of September 7, 1933, CCLC; Copland and Perlis, *Copland 1900 Through 1942*, pp. 207–208.

111. E. E. Cummings, *Complete Poems, 1913–1962* (New York: Harcourt Brace Jovanovich, 1972), pp. 224, 288.

112. Norman, *E. E. Cummings*, p. 139. Milton A. Cohen, *Poet and Painter: The Aesthetics of E. E. Cummings's Early Work* (Detroit: Wayne State University Press, 1987), p. 184.

113. For more on Cummings's esthetics, see Cohen, *Poet and Painter*, pp. 46, 203–209.

114. Norman, *E. E. Cummings*, p. 78.

115. Copland, *The New Music*, p. 46.

116. Copland and Perlis, *Copland 1900 Through 1942*, p. 73.

117. Paul Rosenfeld, "The Americanism of Carlos Chávez," in *By Way of Art* (New York: Coward-McCann, 1928), pp. 279–280.

118. Rosenfeld, "Copland without Jazz," in *By Way of Art*, pp. 266–272.

119. Rosenfeld, "Carlos Chávez," in *An Hour with American Music*, pp. 144–145.

120. Carlos Chávez to Aaron Copland, letter of August 3, 1930, CCLC.

167

121. Copland to Chávez, letter of August 15, 1930, CCLC.

122. Copland to Perlis, interview transcript, box 226/6, p. 209, CCLC.

123. Rita Eder, "Tamayo en Nueva York," in *Rufino Tamayo: 70 Años de Creación* (Mexico City: Museo Rufino Tamayo, 1987), pp. 55–65. See also Julia Smith, *Aaron Copland: His Work and Contribution to American Music* (New York: E. P. Dutton, 1955), p. 44. It is difficult to confirm whether Kuniyoshi met either Tamayo or Copland as cited in the previous references. Kuniyoshi was actually living in Brooklyn at this time, but would certainly have frequented Marsh's studio. Kuniyoshi collected and was influenced by folk art.

124. Robert Goldwater, *Rufino Tamayo* (New York: Quadrangle Press, 1957), pp. 18–19.

125. Adriana Williams, *Covarrubias* (Austin, Tex.: University of Texas Press, 1994), p. 21.

126. George Antheil, *Bad Boy of Music* (New York: Doubleday, Doran, 1945), p. 201.

127. Copland, "Composer from Mexico: Carlos Chávez," in *The New Music*, pp. 145–146; this chapter presents "in somewhat altered form" Copland's article on Chávez that appeared in *The New Republic* on May 2, 1928.

128. Edna Robertson and Sarah Nestor, *Artists of the Canyons and Caminos Santa Fe: The Early Years* (Santa Fe, N. M.: Peregrine Smith, 1976), p. 95.

129. Robertson and Nestor, *Artists of the Canyons*, p. 130.

130. Copland and Perlis, *Copland 1900 Through 1942*, p. 153.

131. Copland and Perlis, *Copland 1900 Through 1942*, p. 153.

132. Thomson, "Aaron Copland," *Modern Music* 9, no. 2 (January–February 1932): 67–73, and Roger Sessions, "An American Evening Abroad," *Modern Music* 4 (November–December 1926): 34. For an overview of identity issues, including that of the "Jewish character" of Copland's music, see Pollack, *Aaron Copland*, pp. 518–531.

133. Copland and Perlis, *Copland 1900 Through 1942*, p. 160.

134. Copland and Perlis, *Copland 1900 Through 1942*, p. 162.

135. Copland and Perlis, *Copland 1900 Through 1942*, p. 162.

136. Clurman, *All People Are Famous*, p. 39.

137. Waldemar George, *Marc Chagall* (Paris: Gallimard, 1928), p. 9; reproduced on p. 59. Some have assigned the date 1918 to this painting.

138. Angelica Zander Rudenstine, *The Guggenheim Museum Collection: Paintings 1880–1945* (New York: Solomon R. Guggenheim Museum, 1976), 1:77.

139. See Gail Levin, "Marsden Hartley, Kandinsky, and Der Blaue Reiter," *Arts Magazine* 52 (November 1977): 156–160, and Gail Levin, "Marsden Hartley's 'Amerika': Between Native American and German Folk Art," in *American Art Review* 5 (winter 1993): 120–125, 170–172.

140. See Smith, *Aaron Copland*, p. 44. At present, it is difficult to pin down when Copland met Kuniyoshi, but given that Smith's book dates from Copland's middle years, when his memory was clear, it seems unlikely that she is in error.

141. Lincoln Kirstein, *Elie Nadelman* (New York: Eakins Press, 1973), pp. 22, 255.

142. Lincoln Kirstein, *The Sculpture of Elie Nadelman* (New York: Museum of Modern Art, 1948).

143. See Gail Levin, *Edward Hopper: An Intimate Biography* (New York: Alfred A. Knopf, 1995), pp. 220–221, 245.

144. Erica Wilson, *Quilts of America* (Birmingham, Ala.: Oxmoor House, 1979), p. 2.

145. See Aaron Copland, "The Composer and His Critic," *Modern Music* 9, no. 4 (May–June 1932): 143; here he stressed that a country must "create its own music." See also Copland, "Composer from Brooklyn," p. 158.

146. See Archie Green, "Thomas Hart Benton's Folk Musicians," *John Edwards Memorial Foundation Quarterly* 12 (summer 1976): 74–90.

147. Today these murals are located in the New Britain (Conn.) Museum of American Art.

148. Thomas Hart Benton, *An Artist in America* (New York: Robert M. McBride, 1937), p. 113.

149. Judith Tick, *Ruth Crawford Seeger: A Composer's Search for American Music* (New York: Oxford University Press, 1997), pp. 235–236. See the three-record 78 r.p.m. album *Saturday Night at Tom Benton's*, Decca Album No. A III.

150. Smith, "Aaron Copland" (Ph.D. diss.), p. 183. Rosenfeld relinquished this position and arranged for Copland to succeed him.

151. See Paul Rosenfeld, "Ex-Reading Room," *The New Republic* (April 12, 1933): 245–246.

152. See, for example, *Copland: Music for Films*, Saint Louis Symphony Orchestra, Leonard Slatkin, BMG/RCA Victor 61699.

153. "U.S. Scene," *Time* 26 (December 24, 1934): 24–27.

154. For his account of his fight with "leftists" in New York, see Thomas Hart Benton, *An American in Art: A Professional and Technical Autobiography* (Lawrence, Kans.: University Press of Kansas, 1969), pp. 164–173.

155. See Thomas Craven, *Modern Art: The Men, the Movements, the Meaning* (New York: Simon & Schuster, 1934), p. 312, where Stieglitz is identified as "a Hoboken Jew without knowledge of, or interest in, the historical American background." Benton (pp. 332–345) is praised as "one of the few living artists, in any department, with a first-rate mind." Rosenfeld was, of course, a strong supporter of Stieglitz and his circle.

156. Benton, *An American in Art*, p. 172.

157. Thomas Hart Benton, "America and/or Alfred Stieglitz," *Common Sense* 4 (January 1935): 22–25, reprinted in Matthew Baigell, ed., *A Thomas Hart Benton Miscellany* (Lawrence, Kans.: University Press of Kansas, 1971), p. 66.

158. Dorothy Norman, *Alfred Stieglitz: An American Seer* (New York: Random House, 1973), p. 196.

159. Clurman, *All People Are Famous*, p. 108. Copland recalled meeting Sykes in 1925 through Paul Rosenfeld in Copland and Perlis, *Copland 1900 Through 1942*, p. 129.

160. Aaron Copland, interview by Paul Falkenberg and Hans Namuth, dirs., in *Alfred Stieglitz*, 1982. A copy of this film is in the collection of the Museum of Modern Art Film Archives, New York.

161. See Sue Davidson Lowe, *Stieglitz: A Memoir/ Biography* (New York: Farrar, Straus & Giroux, 1983), p. 83.

162. Alfred Stieglitz quoted in "291: A Vision Through Photography," in Waldo Frank, Lewis Mumford, Dorothy Norman, Paul Rosenfeld, and Harold Rugg, eds., *America and Alfred Stieglitz: A Collective Portrait* (New York: Literary Guild, 1934), p. 119.

163. Copland to his parents, letter of November 20, 1921, CCLC.

164. Copland to his parents, letter of January 21, 1922, CCLC. See Aaron Copland, "Young Men of Promise," *Modern Music* 3, no. 3 (March–April 1926): 15, where he notes the influence of Bloch on the work of G. Herbert Elwell.

165. Copland and Perlis, *Copland 1900 Through 1942*, pp. 117, 190.

166. See Marilyn J. Ziffrin, *Carl Ruggles: Composer, Painter, and Storyteller* (Urbana, Ill.: University of Illinois Press, 1994), pp. 74–75.

167. Ziffrin, *Carl Ruggles*, p. 243.

168. Tick, *Ruth Crawford Seeger*, p. 111. Crawford Seeger told Ruggles in December 1929, just months after the great stock market crash, "You are American if you're American in spirit . . . Amalgamation will be a great thing. Out of all the races will spring the true American."

169. Ziffrin, *Carl Ruggles*, pp. 52–60.

170. Zuck, *A History of Musical Americanism*, p. 112.

171. Benton, *An American in Art*, p. 54.

172. Thomas Hart Benton to Carl Ruggles, quoted in Ziffrin, *Carl Ruggles*, p. 143.

173. Frank, *Our America*, p. 4.

174. Paul Rosenfeld, "American Painting," *The Dial* 71 (December 1921): 649–670.

175. Edward Hopper, "John Sloan and the Philadelphians," *The Arts* 2 (April 1927): 177–178.

176. Georgia O'Keeffe, *Georgia O'Keeffe* (New York: Viking Press, 1976), n.p.; quote appears opposite plate 58.

177. Georgia O'Keeffe to Aaron Copland, letter of July 19, 1968, in Jack Cowart, Juan Hamilton, and Sarah Greenough, eds., *Georgia O'Keeffe: Art and Letters* (Washington, D.C.: National Gallery of Art, 1981), p. 269.

178. See Gail Levin, "Die Musik in der Frühen Amerikanischen Abstraktion," in Karin v. Maur, *Vom Klang der Bilder: Die Musik in der Kunst des 20. Jahrhunderts* (Munich: Prestel, 1985), pp. 368–373.

179. See Judith K. Zilczer, "Synaesthesia and Popular Culture: Arthur Dove, Gershwin, and the 'Rhapsody in Blue,'" *Art Journal* 44 (winter 1984): 361–366.

180. Copland and Perlis, *Copland 1900 Through 1942*, p. 130.

181. Copland to Don Gold, 1958, interview transcript, CCLC, cited in Pollack, *Aaron Copland*, pp. 117, 552.

182. Copland to Paul Strand, letter of August 6, 1974, CCLC, cited in Pollack, *Aaron Copland*, p. 102.

183. Copland and Perlis, *Copland 1900 Through 1942*, p. 214.

184. Rosenfeld, "The Americanism of Carlos Chávez," p. 282.

185. Chávez quoted in Robert L. Parker, *Carlos Chávez: Mexico's Modern-Day Orpheus* (Boston: Twayne, 1983), p. 6.

186. Copland, "Composer from Mexico," p. 148.

187. John Martin, "Mexican Ballet in World Premiere," *New York Times*, April 1, 1932.

188. See Diego Rivera and Gladys March, *My Art, My Life* (New York: Citadel Press, 1960), p. 159.

189. See Roberto García Morillo, *Carlos Chávez: Vida y Obra* (Mexico City and Buenos Aires: Fondo de Cultura Económica, 1960), p. 68.

190. Copland and Perlis, *Copland 1900 Through 1942*, p. 216.

191. Aaron Copland, "The Story Behind *El Salón México*," c. 1939; this published article appears in CCLC, but not in Joann Skowronski, *Aaron Copland: A Bio-bibliography* (Westport, Conn.: Greenwood Press, 1985). Pollack, *Aaron Copland*, p. 625, note 22, dates the article c. 1939 and identifies it as having been "written on the occasion of the 1939 Victor release of the work." See Anita Brenner, *Your Mexican Holiday, A Modern Guide* (New York: G. P. Putnam's Sons, 1932), p. 59.

192. James Oles, *South of the Border: Mexico in the American Imagination, 1914–1947* (Washington, D.C.: Smithsonian Institution Press, 1993), p. 121.

193. Copland to Mary Lescaze, letter of January 13, 1933, excerpted in Copland and Perlis, *Copland 1900 Through 1942*, p. 216.

194. Michael E. Hoffman, ed., *Paul Strand: Sixty Years of Photographs* (New York: Aperture, 1976), p. 155.

195. See, for example, Marsden Hartley's "Twilight of the Acrobat," *The Seven Arts* 1 (January 1917): 287–291, and "Albert Pinkham Ryder," *The Seven Arts* 2 (May 1917): 93–96.

196. See Gail Levin, "Marsden Hartley and Mysticism," *Arts Magazine* 60 (November 1985): 16–21. Richard Hennessy, interview by author, May 2000.

197. Copland and Perlis, *Copland Since 1943*, p. 53.

198. Marsden Hartley, "The Red Man," in *Marsden Hartley, Adventures in the Arts* (New York: Boni & Liveright, 1921), p. 15.

199. Gertrude Stein, *The Autobiography of Alice B. Toklas* (New York: Harcourt, Brace, 1933), p. 309.

200. Copland and Perlis, *Copland 1900 Through 1942*, p. 33.

201. Harold Clurman to Copland, letter of May 24, 1932, in Copland and Perlis, *Copland 1900 Through 1942*, p. 219.

202. Aaron Copland, "Workers Sing!," *New Masses* (November 9, 1934): 28–29.

203. James Dennis, interview with Grant Wood's assistant, in *Grant Wood* (New York: Viking Press, 1975), p. 239, note 1.

204. Copland's "Into the Streets May First" was published in *New Masses* 11, no. 5 (May 1, 1934): 16–17.

205. Aaron Copland to Carlos Chávez, letter of September 30, 1935, Chávez papers, The New York Public Library. See also Copland's review of *Discoveries of a Music Critic*, by Paul Rosenfeld, in *The New Republic* (April 15, 1936): 291; here, Copland disagrees with Rosenfeld's assertion that "the living communist faith and idea are not a part of any genial living composer."

206. Pollack, *Aaron Copland*, p. 272; Copland and Perlis, *Copland Since 1943*, p. 189.

207. See Pollack, *Aaron Copland*, pp. 270–287, and Terry Teachout, "Fanfare for Aaron Copland," in *Commentary* 103 (January 1997): 56–61.

208. Patrick Marnham, *Dreaming with His Eyes Open: A Life of Diego Rivera* (New York: Alfred A. Knopf, 1998), pp. 259, 277–294. Rivera gave Trotsky safe harbor in his home in Mexico until he discovered that Trotsky had betrayed him by having an affair with his wife; at that point Rivera turned on the exiled Russian leader.

209. This description of the mural is from "Rockefellers Ban Lenin in RCA Mural and Dismiss Rivera," *New York Times*, April 10, 1933, art. 10, reprinted in Irene Herner de Larrea et al., *Diego Rivera: Peraison Perdido en Rockefeller Center* (Mexico City: Edicupes, 1986), p. 78.

210. Walter Pach, "Rockefeller, Rivera, and Art," *Harper's Magazine* (September 1933), art. 63, in de Larrea, *Diego Rivera*, p. 150.

211. I am grateful to Patrick Marnham for this information, which is among the Bertram Wolfe papers in the Hoover Institution Archives, Stanford, California, box BW 113-8.

212. *A Life of Diego Rivera*, p. 259.

213. Erik Johns in conversation with author, January 30, 2000.

214. See Tick, *Ruth Crawford Seeger*, pp. 191–193.

215. Inscribed in *Ruth Page Kreutzberg*, a book of her work, given to Copland for Christmas in 1934: "To Aaron the American composer with my esteem, my gratitude and my love Ruth." Collection of Erik Johns.

216. Copland and Perlis, *Copland 1900 Through 1942*, p. 234.

217. See Frances K. Pohl, *Ben Shahn: New Deal Artist in a Cold War Climate, 1947–1954* (Austin, Tex.: University of Texas Press, 1989).

218. Aaron Copland, "Composer from Brooklyn," p. 161.

169

219. Copland quoted in Pollack, *Aaron Copland*, p. 298.

220. Edwin Denby to Aaron Copland, undated letter of 1943, CCLC; Willem de Kooning married Elaine Fried in 1943 and Max Margulis was best man.

221. Elaine de Kooning to Edvard Lieber, in conversation between author and Edvard Lieber, August 7, 1999.

222. Elaine de Kooning recounted this to Edvard Lieber, who recorded it and other recollections; relayed in conversation between Lieber and author, August 7, 1999.

223. Erik Johns, interview by author, January 20, 2000.

224. Copland, "The Composer in Industrial America," pp. 103–104.

225. See Aaron Copland, "Notes on a Cowboy Ballet," CCLC.

226. Warren A. Beck, *New Mexico: A History of Four Centuries* (Norman, Okla.: University of Oklahoma Press, 1962), p. 333.

227. Nicholas Fox Weber, *Patron Saints: Five Rebels Who Opened America to a New Art, 1928–1943* (New York: Alfred A. Knopf, 1992), p. 181.

228. Rosamund (Peggy) Bernier in Copland and Perlis, *Copland 1900 Through 1942*, p. 267.

229. Virgil Thomson, *Virgil Thomson: An Autobiography by Virgil Thomson* (New York: Alfred A. Knopf, 1966), p. 215.

230. Robert Cornfield and William Mackay, *Edwin Denby: Dance Writings* (New York: Alfred A. Knopf, 1986), p. 27.

231. Copland and Perlis, *Copland 1900 Through 1942*, p. 290.

232. Edwin Denby to Aaron Copland, letter of November 18, 1939, CCLC.

233. Denby to Copland, letter of November 18, 1939, CCLC.

234. William Lescaze to Aaron Copland, letter of October 1, 1942, CCLC. William Lescaze, *On Being an Architect* (New York: G. P. Putnam's Sons, 1942).

235. Lescaze, *On Being an Architect*, p. 27.

236. Clurman, *All People Are Famous*, p. 109.

237. Copland and Perlis, *Copland Since 1943*, p. 233.

238. Benton, *An Artist in America*, p. 186.

239. The director Spike Lee included "John Henry" among the Copland scores he used in his film *He Got Game* (1998).

240. The statement of Congressman Fred E. Busbey of Illinois questioning Copland's political associations appeared in the *Congressional Record*. See *Proceedings and Debates of the Eighty-third Congress, First Session*, appendix, vol. 99, part 9 (January 3, 1953–March 23, 1953), pp. 169–71.

241. Pollack, *Aaron Copland*, pp. 259, 264–265.

242. Clifford Odets to Aaron Copland, undated letter of 1951, CCLC.

243. Clurman, *All People Are Famous*, p. 123.

244. Copland to Odets, letter of October 18, 1951, CCLC.

245. Odets to Copland, letter of November 8, 1953; see also Odets to Copland, letter of September 22, 1952; both in CCLC.

246. Aaron Copland, Diaries, September 20, 1955, CCLC, quoted in Pollack, *Aaron Copland*, p. 463.

247. Copland to Phillip Ramey, interview published on cover of *Copland Conducts Copland*, London Symphony Orchestra, Columbia Masterworks, 1979.

248. Carl Sandburg, *Abraham Lincoln: The Prairie Years*, 2 vols. (New York: Harcourt, Brace, 1926), and *Abraham Lincoln: The War Years*, 4 vols. (New York: Harcourt, Brace, 1939).

249. Agnes de Mille in Copland and Perlis, *Copland 1900 Through 1942*, p. 357.

250. John A. Lomax and Alan Lomax, *Our Singing Country: A Second Volume of American Ballads and Folk Songs* (New York: Macmillan, 1941).

251. Holger Cahill, *American Folk Art: The Art of the Common Man in America, 1750–1900* (New York: Museum of Modern Art, 1932), pp. 26–27.

252. See Cécile Whiting, *Antifascism in American Art* (New Haven: Yale University Press, 1989), pp. 142–145.

253. Cahill, *American Folk Art*, p. 28.

254. Aaron Copland, "Composer from Brooklyn," p. 161.

255. Copland and Perlis, *Copland Since 1943*, p. 68.

256. Martha Graham, "House of Victory," script sent to Copland May 16, 1943, CCLC.

257. Graham, "House of Victory," p. 5, CCLC.

258. Graham, "House of Victory," p. 8, CCLC.

259. From the script version entitled "Name?," sent by Graham to Copland in summer 1943, CCLC.

260. Grant Wood, in "Interview with Grant Wood," *Cedar Rapids Gazette*, June 29, 1941, quoted in James M. Dennis, *Renegade Regionalists* (Madison, Wisc.: University of Wisconsin Press, 1998), p. 259. Graham also may have seen this work reproduced in *The Art Digest* (April 1, 1942): 6.

261. Grant Wood, quoted in a statement of January 2, 1940, in Whiting, *Antifascism in American Art*, p. 100.

262. Howard Mumford Jones, "Patriotism—But How?" *The Atlantic Monthly* 162 (November 1938): 585–592.

263. See Francis X. Clines, "Appalachia's Treasures Go on the Global Market," *New York Times*, March 12, 2000, p. 18; the article describes the current global marketing plan of quilt makers in an Appalachian town in Virginia.

264. Brom Weber, ed., *The Complete Poems and Selected Letters and Prose of Hart Crane* (New York: Anchor Books, 1966), pp. 72, 52.

265. Martha Graham to Aaron Copland, script, July 10, 1943, CCLC. William Carlos Williams, *In the American Grain* (New York: New Directions, 1925).

266. Copland and Perlis, *Copland Since 1943*, pp. 34, 53.

267. Copland and Perlis, *Copland Since 1943*, p. 53. See above for the discussion of Copland's planned elegy to Crane.

268. Edward D. Andrews, *The Gift to Be Simple: Songs, Dances and Rituals of the American Shakers* (New York: J. J. Augustin, 1940), p. 136.

269. Constance Rourke, *The Roots of American Culture and Other Essays*, ed. Van Wyck Brooks (New York: Harcourt, Brace, 1942), p. 219.

270. Constance Rourke, *Charles Sheeler: Artist in the American Tradition* (New York: Harcourt, Brace, 1938).

271. Copland and Perlis, *Copland Since 1943*, p. 32.

272. Copland to Phillip Ramey, interview published on cover of *Copland Conducts Copland: First Recording of the Original Version, Appalachian Spring (Complete Ballet)*, Columbia Chamber Orchestra, CBS Modern American Music Series, 1974.

273. Isamu Noguchi in Copland and Perlis, *Copland Since 1943*, p. 53.

274. Ted Shawn, *The American Ballet* (New York: Henry Holt, 1926), pp. 58–61.

275. Shawn, *The American Ballet*, p. 57.

276. Agnes de Mille in Copland and Perlis, *Copland 1900 Through 1942*, pp. 359–360.

277. Frank, *Our America*, p. 214.

278. Copland and Perlis, *Copland 1900 Through 1942*, p. 290.

279. Copland and Perlis, *Copland 1900 Through 1942*, p. 297.

280. Aaron Copland, "Second Thoughts on Hollywood," *Modern Music* 17, no. 3 (March–April 1940): 141–147; and Aaron Copland, "The Aim of Music for Films," *New York Times*, March 10, 1940, sec. 2, p. 7.

281. Copland, "Second Thoughts on Hollywood," pp. 142–143.

282. Copland and Perlis, *Copland Since 1943*, p. 21.

283. Spike Lee, "Why Aaron Copland?," liner notes to *He Got Game: Spike Lee Presents the Music of Aaron Copland*, motion picture soundtrack, Sony Classical SK60593, 1998.

284. Copland and Perlis, *Copland Since 1943*, p. 158.

285. Copland and Perlis, *Copland Since 1943*; according to Perlis, "*The Dickinson Songs* predated a more reliable variorum edition" issued in 1955. Copland used an edition by Martha Dickinson Bianchi and Alfred Leete Hampson (1914–1930), which contained errors.

286. Pollack, *Aaron Copland*, p. 440.

287. James Agee and Walker Evans, *Let Us Now Praise Famous Men* (Boston: Houghton Mifflin, 1941).

288. Aaron Copland, *The Tender Land: Opera in Three Acts*. Libretto by Horace Everett (New York: Boosey & Hawkes, 1956).

289. Copland and Perlis, *Copland Since 1943*, p. 389.

290. Humphrey Burton, *Leonard Bernstein* (New York: Doubleday, 1994), p. 59.

291. The sculpture is 54 feet long, 43 feet high, has 20- and 30-foot arches, and weighs 42 tons.

292. Erik Johns, interview by author, January 20, 2000.

293. Copland and Perlis, *Copland Since 1943*, p. 360.

294. Alexander Calder as quoted in *In Commemoration: The Dedication of "La Grande Vitesse" by Alexander Calder*, program for dedication at Vandenberg Center, Grand Rapids, Michigan, June 14, 1969, p. 7.

295. Robert Osborn, "Calder's International Monuments," *Art in America* (March–April 1969), reprinted in *In Commemoration*, p. 5.

296. Aaron Copland, "The Ives Case," in *The New Music*, p. 114.

297. Pollack, *Aaron Copland*, pp. 514–515.

298. This event was incorrectly identified as his birthday party in Jane K. Bledsoe, *Elaine de Kooning* (Athens, Ga.: Georgia Museum of Art, 1993), p. 18. This was confirmed by Edvard Lieber and Vivian Perlis in conversations with the author, August 13, 1999.

299. Louise Nevelson to Aaron Copland, letter of October 30, 1984, CCLC.

300. See Pollack, *Aaron Copland*, pp. 245, 250–251.

301. The 1957 sketch (pencil on cardboard, 11 x 15") is now in the CCLC.

302. Pollack, *Aaron Copland*, pp. 542–543.

303. The inscription is dated August 8, 1980. Collection of Erik Johns.

304. Edvard Lieber, letter to author, November 14, 1999.

305. *Copland Conducts Copland*, London Symphony Orchestra, Columbia Masterworks, 1975. This album includes *Our Town, An Outdoor Overture, Quiet City*, and *Two Pieces for String Orchestra*, but not *Appalachian Spring*.

306. *Cadenzas and Variations*, New World Records, 1981. This was a debut recording by violinist Gregory Fulkerson with pianists Alan Feinberg and Robert Shannon.

307. Aaron Copland, *Third Symphony*, London Symphony Orchestra, Everest Records SDBR 3018, 1959. For a discussion of Copland's *Third Symphony* and its reception, see Pollack, *Aaron Copland*, pp. 410–419.

PICTURING AARON COPLAND

1. Minna Lederman Daniel, quoted in Aaron Copland and Vivian Perlis, *Copland 1900 Through 1942*, p. 112.

2. Rhoda Sherbell, interview by author, January 30, 2000.

171

The Music of Aaron Copland

Judith Tick

1. Leonard Bernstein, "Copland at 79," in *Findings* (New York: Simon & Schuster, 1982), p. 337.

2. Aaron Copland, *Our New Music* (New York: McGraw Hill, 1941), p. 79.

3. "imposed simplicity": Copland in *Our New Music*, p. 229; "the way out of isolation": Aaron Copland and Vivian Perlis, *Copland 1900 Through 1942* (New York: St. Martin's Press, 1984), p. 279.

4. Copland and Perlis, *Copland 1900 Through 1942*, p. 251.

5. "La part de Dieu" and "unconscious part," in Aaron Copland, *Music and Imagination* (Cambridge: Harvard University Press, 1952), p. 46; "What that particular work . . .": Copland and Perlis, *Copland 1900 Through 1942*, p. 166.

6. Copland, *Our New Music*, p. 212.

7. Copland, *Music and Imagination*, pp. 97–99. This book consists of the six Charles Eliot Norton Lectures Copland delivered at Harvard University in fall 1951 and spring 1952.

8. Howard Pollack, *Aaron Copland: The Life and Work of an Uncommon Man* (New York: Henry Holt, 1999), p. 23

9. Copland and Perlis, *Copland 1900 Through 1942*, p. 16.

10. Pollack, *Aaron Copland*, pp. 34–35.

11. Reid Badger, *A Life in Ragtime: A Biography of James Reese Europe* (New York: Oxford University Press, 1995), p. 46. Adrienne Fried Block, "Dvořák's Long American Reach" in John Tibbetts, ed., *Dvořák in America, 1892–1895* (Portland, Ore.: Amadeus Press, 1993), pp. 157–181.

12. Copland and Perlis, *Copland 1900 Through 1942*, p. 32.

13. Julia Smith, *Aaron Copland: His Work and Contribution to American Music* (New York: E. P. Dutton, 1955), p. 33.

14. Claire Reis, *Composers, Conductors and Critics* (New York: Oxford University Press, 1955), p. 36.

15. Glenn Watkins, *Soundings* (New York: Schirmer Books, 1995), pp. 236ff.

16. Copland, *Music and Imagination*, p. 98.

17. Copland and Perlis, *Copland 1900 Through 1942*, p. 36.

18. David Metzer, "'Spurned Love': Eroticism and Abstraction in the Early Works of Aaron Copland,"

The Journal of Musicology 15, no. 4 (fall 1997): 418–419.

19. The title *Moods for Piano Solo* appears on the title page of the manuscript of this set, along with the French title *Trois Esquisses*. The internal titles are in English, as follows: "Embittered," "Wistful," and "Jazzy."

20. Copland and Perlis, *Copland 1900 Through 1942*, p. 20.

21. Pollack, *Aaron Copland*, p. 44.

22. "My Buddy" has lyrics by Gus Kahn and music by Walter Donaldson. See Ellen Donaldson and Ronny Schiff, eds., *The Walter Donaldson Songbook* (New York: Donaldson Publishing, 1988), pp. 37–39. The reference to "My Buddy" is pointed out by Phillip Ramey in his liner notes to the CD *The Young Pioneers: The Complete Music for Solo Piano*, Leo Smit, Sony SM2K 66345, 1994. There is some confusion about dating "Jazzy," which quotes from "My Buddy," a tune supposedly written in 1922 but with a manuscript date of July 1921. Copland Collection, Library of Congress [hereafter CCLC].

23. Pollack, *Aaron Copland*, p. 44.

24. Rubin Goldmark to Aaron Copland, letter of August 26, 1921, cited in Julia Smith, *Aaron Copland*, p. 42.

25. Cole Gagne and Tracy Caras, eds., *Soundpieces: Interviews with American Composers* (Metuchen, N.J.: Scarecrow Press, 1982), p. 112.

26. Phillip Ramey, "Copland and the Dance," *Ballet News* 2, no. 5 (1980): 10.

27. Pollack, *Aaron Copland*, pp. 122ff.

28. Anthony Tommasini, *Virgil Thomson: Composer on the Aisle* (New York: W. W. Norton, 1997), p. 98.

29. Copland and Perlis, *Copland 1900 Through 1942*, p. 91.

30. Copland, *Music and Imagination*, pp. 37–38.

31. Aaron Copland, "The Art of Darius Milhaud," *The Saturday Review of Literature* 6, no. 26 (1948): 43.

32. Copland and Perlis, *Copland 1900 Through 1942*, p. 226.

33. Oliver Knussen reconstructed *Grohg* and recorded it with the Cleveland Orchestra; Argo 443 203-2, 1994.

34. Aaron Copland, *What to Listen for in Music* (New York: McGraw-Hill, 1939), p. 75.

35. Copland, *What to Listen for in Music*, p. 44.

36. Copland, *What to Listen for in Music*, p. 45.

37. Copland and Perlis, *Copland 1900 Through 1942*, pp. 84–86.

38. Copland, *Music and Imagination*, p. 99.

39. Copland, *Music and Imagination*, p. 98.

40. Copland and Perlis, *Copland 1900 Through 1942*, p. 134.

41. Rachmaninoff quoted in Oliver Daniel, *Stokowski: A Counterpoint of View* (New York: Dodd, Mead, 1982), p. 300.

42. Paul Rosenfeld, *An Hour with American Music* (Philadelphia: J. B. Lippincott, 1929), pp. 26–27.

43. Carol J. Oja, "Cos Cob Press and the American Composer," *Notes* 44, no. 4 (December 1988): 227–252.

44. Frank quoted in Carol J. Oja, "Women Patrons and Crusaders for Modernist Music," in Ralph P. Locke and Cyrilla Barr, eds., *Cultivating Music in America: Women Patrons and Activists Since 1860* (Berkeley: University of California Press, 1997), p. 245.

45. Oja, "Women Patrons and Crusaders," p. 245.

46. Thomas DeLong, *Pops: Paul Whiteman, King of Jazz* (Piscataway, N. J.: New Century Publishers, 1983), pp. 76–77.

47. Copland and Perlis, *Copland 1900 Through 1942*, p. 95.

48. For the description of jazz as "Negro music seen through the eyes of Tin Pan Alley Jews," see Henry Cowell, "Bericht aus Amerika: Amerikanische Musik,"

in *Melos* 9 (August–September 1930): 364. Reports by Cowell, an American composer, were translated into German.

49. Rosenfeld, *An Hour with American Music*, p. 11.

50. Joel A. Rogers, "Jazz at Home," originally published in *Survey Graphic* (March 1925), reprinted in Alain Locke, ed., *The New Negro: An Interpretation* (New York: A. & C. Boni, 1926); Rogers in David Levering Lewis, ed., *The Portable Harlem Renaissance Reader* (New York: Penguin, 1994), pp. 54–56. For a discussion of the conflicting attitudes toward jazz among black cultural critics and black music historians, see Guthrie P. Ramsey Jr., "Cosmopolitan or Provincial? Ideology in Early Black Music Historiography, 1867–1940," *Black Music Research Journal* 16, no. 1 (spring 1996): 26–27.

51. Pollack, *Aaron Copland*, p. 113.

52. *Modern Music* 4 (January–February 1927): 9–14.

53. "The Jazz Problem" was the lead story featured on the cover of the August 1924 issue of *The Etude Music Magazine*, which included in its pages a symposium of musicians' responses. For a sampling of opinions from this issue, see Robert Walser, ed., *Keeping Time: Readings in Jazz History* (New York: Oxford University Press, 1999), pp. 41–54.

54. Aaron Copland, handwritten lecture notes for a course on modern music, CCLC. The notes are undated but are definitely from before 1937, because George Gershwin is listed in them as a living composer.

55. "The Sidewalks of New York," by Charles B. Lawlor and James W. Blake, was published in 1894. Copland used the opening melody of its famous first line, "East Side, West Side."

56. Pollack, *Aaron Copland*, p. 130.

57. Pollack, *Aaron Copland*, p. 130.

58. Gerald Bordman, *American Musical Theatre: A Chronicle*, 2d ed. (New York: Oxford University Press, 1992), p. 397.

59. Aaron Copland, 1937, quoted in Barbara Zuck, *A History of Musical Americanism* (Ann Arbor, Mich.: UMI Research Press, 1978), p. 251.

60. Copland and Perlis, *Copland 1900 Through 1942*, p. 119.

61. Copland and Perlis, *Copland 1900 Through 1942*, p. 131.

62. Undated letter from Aaron Copland to Nicolas Slonimsky, in Gertrude Norman and Miriam L. Schrifte, eds., *Letters of Composers: An Anthology, 1603–1945* (New York: Alfred A. Knopf, 1946), p. 401.

63. Pollack, *Aaron Copland*, pp. 142–143 and note 3, p. 593.

64. S. Ansky, *The Dybbuk*, trans. Henry Alsberg and Winifred Katzin (New York: Liveright, 1926).

65. Nahma Sandrow, *Vagabond Stars: A World History of Yiddish Theater* (New York: Harper & Row, 1977), pp. 218–219. The play was particularly associated with two troupes, the Vilna Troupe and Habima, both famous for their expressionistic approaches to their productions.

66. Copland and Perlis, *Copland 1900 Through 1942*, p. 162.

67. Copland and Perlis, *Copland 1900 Through 1942*, p. 162.

68. "Copland Remembered," *Opera News* 55, no. 2 (February 1991): 33.

69. Pollack, *Aaron Copland*, p. 461.

70. Gagne and Caras, *Soundpieces*, p. 103.

71. Copland and Perlis, *Copland 1900 Through 1942*, p. 183.

72. Aaron Copland, *The New Music: 1900–1960* (New York: W. W. Norton, 1968), p. 161.

73. Richard Pells, *Radical Visions and American Dreams: Cultural and Social Thought in the Depression Years*

(Middletown, Conn.: Wesleyan University Press, 1973), pp. 158–159.

74. Aaron Copland, "The Composer and His Critic," *Modern Music* 9, no. 4 (May–June 1932): 144.

75. Copland and Perlis, *Copland 1900 Through 1942*, p. 226.

76. Pollack, *Aaron Copland*, p. 296.

77. For a discussion of music as a weapon in the class struggle, see Judith Tick, *Ruth Crawford Seeger: A Composer's Search for American Music* (New York: Oxford University Press, 1997), pp. 190ff; William Lichtenwanger, *The Music of Henry Cowell: A Descriptive Catalog* (New York: Institute for Studies in American Music, 1986), pp. 140–141.

78. Carol J. Oja, "Marc Blitzstein's *The Cradle Will Rock* and Mass-Song Style of the 1930s," *Musical Quarterly* 73, no. 4 (1989): 446.

79. Copland and Perlis, *Copland 1900 Through 1942*, p. 225.

80. Pollack, *Aaron Copland*, p. 304.

81. Pollack, *Aaron Copland*, pp. 305–306.

82. Copland and Perlis, *Copland 1900 Through 1942*, p. 237.

83. Copland, *Our New Music*, p. 229.

84. Linda Danly, ed., *Hugo Friedhofer: The Best Years of His Life* (Lanham, Md.: Scarecrow Press, 1999), p. 84.

85. Paul Rosenfeld, "Folksong and Culture-Politics," *Modern Music* 17, no. 1 (October–November 1939): 20–22.

86. Tick, *Ruth Crawford Seeger*, p. 258.

87. Charles Louis Seeger, "Grass Roots for American Composers," *Modern Music* 16, no. 3 (March–April 1939): 143–149.

88. Darius Milhaud, *Notes Without Music* (New York: Alfred A. Knopf, 1952), p. 311.

89. Pollack, *Aaron Copland*, p. 308.

90. Copland and Perlis, *Copland 1900 Through 1942*, p. 246.

91. Copland and Perlis, *Copland 1900 Through 1942*, p. 246.

92. Pollack, *Aaron Copland*, p. 320.

93. Pollack, *Aaron Copland*, p. 320.

94. Pollack, *Aaron Copland*, p. 320.

95. Aaron Copland to Arthur Berger, letter of April 10, 1943, in Norman and Schrifte, *Letters of Composers*, p. 403.

96. Copland, *Music and Imagination*, p. 109.

97. Copland, *Music and Imagination*, pp. 103–104.

98. Peter Evans, "The Thematic Technique of Copland's Recent Works," *Tempo* 59 (1959): 3.

99. The term "Westering" is spoken by the grandfather in the film version of Steinbeck's *The Red Pony*.

100. Tick, *Ruth Crawford Seeger*, p. 242.

101. Charles Seeger, "Contrapuntal Style in Three-voice Shape-note Hymns," *Musical Quarterly* 26, no. 4 (October 1940): 493.

102. Aaron Copland, "New Records," *Modern Music* 16, no. 3 (March–April 1939): 186.

103. Arthur Berger, *Aaron Copland* (New York: Oxford University Press, 1953), p. 60.

104. Aaron Copland and Vivian Perlis, *Copland Since 1943* (New York: St. Martin's Press, 1989), p. 23.

105. Israel Citkowitz, unpublished untitled essay, CCLC.

106. Pollack, *Aaron Copland*, p. 395.

107. Harold Clurman to Aaron Copland, letter of March 16, 1943, CCLC.

108. Wilfrid Mellers, *Music in a New Found Land: Themes and Developments in the History of American Music*, rev. ed. (New York: Oxford University Press, 1987), p. 92.

109. Copland and Perlis, *Copland 1900 Through 1942*, p. 332.

110. Phillip Ramey, "Copland and the Dance," *Ballet News* 2, no. 5 (1980): 12.

111. Copland and Perlis, *Copland Since 1943*, p. 32.

112. Copland and Perlis, *Copland Since 1943*, pp. 40–41.

113. Copland and Perlis, *Copland 1900 Through 1942*, pp. 356–357.

114. Dancer Pearl Lang, quoted in Copland and Perlis, *Copland Since 1943*, pp. 43–44.

115. Jan Swafford, *Charles Ives: A Life with Music* (New York: W. W. Norton, 1996), p. 399.

116. Pollack, *Aaron Copland*, p. 469.

117. Charles Ives wrote a set of Harvest Home Chorales. See Swafford, *Charles Ives*, pp. 161ff.

118. Andrew Clements, "Western Europe, 1945–1970," in Robert Morgan, ed., *Modern Times: From World War I to the Present* (Englewood Cliffs, N.J.: Prentice-Hall, 1994), p. 260.

119. Pollack, *Aaron Copland*, p. 461.

120. Copland as quoted in Pollack, *Aaron Copland*, pp. 446, 448.

121. Copland, *Music and Imagination*, p. 66.

122. Copland and Perlis, *Copland Since 1943*, p. 350.

123. Copland and Perlis, *Copland Since 1943*, p. 242.

124. Copland as quoted by Phillip Ramey in liner notes to *The Young Pioneers*, Sony SM2K 66345.

125. Preface to the score of *Twelve Poems of Emily Dickinson*.

126. Guy Rotella, *Reading and Writing Nature* (Boston: Northeastern University Press, 1991), p. 34.

127. Copland and Perlis, *Copland Since 1943*, p. 162.

128. Copland and Perlis, *Copland Since 1943*, p. 158.

INDEX

174